The Native American Warrior

WARRIORS OF THE WORLD

The Native American Warrior

1500–1890 CE

CHRIS McNAB

THOMAS DUNNE BOOKS
ST. MARTIN'S PRESS ☙ NEW YORK

Thomas Dunne Books
An imprint of St. Martin's Press

WARRIORS OF THE WORLD
THE NATIVE AMERICAN WARRIOR 1500–1890 CE

For information, address
St. Martin's Press, 175 Fifth Avenue,
New York, N.Y. 10010.

www.thomasdunnebooks.com
www.stmartins.com

Library of Congress Cataloging-in-Publication Data
on file at the Library of Congress

ISBN-13: 978-0-312-59689-7

Editorial and design by
Amber Books Ltd
Bradley's Close
74–77 White Lion Street
London N1 9PF
United Kingdom
www.amberbooks.co.uk

Project editor: Michael Spilling
Design: Joe Conneally
Picture research: Natascha Spargo
Maps and illustrations: JB Illustrations

Printed in China

10 9 8 7 6 5 4 3 2 1

PICTURE CREDITS:
All maps and black-and-white line artworks produced by JB Illustrations © Amber Books

AKG Images: 47 & 75 (North Wind Picture Archives), 162 (North Wind Picture Archives)
Alamy: 98tr (North Wind Picture Archives)
Art Archive: 128/129 (William E. Weiss/Buffalo Bill Historical Center), 194 (Buffalo Bill Historical Center)
Bridgeman Art Library: 88/89 (Peter Newark American Pictures), 104/105bl (Peter Newark American Pictures), 120 (Look & Learn),
133 (Peter Newark American Pictures), 135 & 151 (Look & Learn), 174 & 197 (Peter Newark American Pictures)
Corbis: 19 & 20 (Bettmann), 22t (Werner Forman Archive), 32 (Robert Wagenhoffer), 39 (Marilyn Angel Wynn/Nativestock Pictures),
42, 55 (Medford Historical Society Collection), 56/57 (Historical Picture Archive), 58 (Historical Picture Archive), 62 (Nik Wheeler),
63, 64, 83 (Bettmann), 86 (Peter Harholdt), 112, 137, 143, 146, 152, 157, 158, 159, 160 (Bettmann), 161 (Poodles Rock), 165tr, 165b
(Tria Giovan), 176, 184 (Bettmann), 192 (Werner Forman Archive), 206, 209, 210, 211, 214/215 (Bettmann)
Dorling Kindersley: 105t (Geoff Brightling)
Getty Images: 8 (Bridgeman Art Library), 11 (Roger Viollet), 15 (Joe Sohm/Visions of America), 25 (Time & Life Pictures),
29 (Marilyn Angel Wynn/Nativestock Pictures), 36, 48 & 74 (Bridgeman Art Library), 78br (Science & Society Picture Library),
79tr & 97 (Hulton Archive), 140 & 145 (Time & Life Pictures), 148 (SuperStock), 150 (Bridgeman Art Library),
170/171 (Hulton Archive), 177 (Hulton Archive), 178 (Marilyn Angel Wynn/Nativestock Pictures), 193 (Bridgeman Art Library),
204/205, 207 (Hulton Archive)
iStockphoto: 153 (Duncan Walker)
Library of Congress: 9, 12/13, 17, 27tr, 41, 45, 49, 50/51, 54, 59, 65tl, 65b, 70, 72tr, 76, 85tl, 85br, 98bl, 100, 106, 109tl,
111, 115, 117, 118, 119, 121, 125, 127tr, 130, 139, 141 (both), 144, 154/155, 156, 163, 164, 167, 168 & 169 (all),
180 (both), 183 & 183 (both), 185, 187, 188, 195, 198/199, 200, 208
Mary Evans Picture Library: 81, 147, 181
Photos.com: 78/79tl, 90, 91, 109b, 127b, 172, 175
Photoshot: 6/7 (World Illustrated), 22bl & 113 (UPPA), 179 (UPPA)
Public Domain: 72bl, 122
TopFoto: 102/103 (Granger Collection), 138 & 191 (Granger Collection)
U.S. Department of Defense: 213
Werner Forman Archive: 27b (Ohio State Museum), 202 (Anthropological Museum of Lomonosov, Moscow)

CONTENTS

Introduction

'Hearing the noise of some guns, we looked out; several houses were burning and the smoke ascending to heaven. There were five persons taken in one house; the father and the mother and a suckling child they knocked on the head; the other two they took and carried away alive. There were two others, who, being out of their garrison upon some occasion, were set upon; one was knocked on the head, the other escaped. Another there was who, running along, was shot and wounded, and fell down; he begged of them his life, promising them money (as they told me), but they would not hearken to him, but knocked him on the head, and stripped him naked, and split open his bowels ... Thus these murderous wretches went on burning and destroying before them.'

– *Mary Rowlandson (1682)*

This quotation comes from Mary Rowlandson, wife of the minister of Lancaster, Massachusetts, who on 10 February 1675 witnessed the destruction of her town by Narragansett, Wampanoag and Nashaway/Nipmuc Indians. The Indians left 13 dead and took 24 people captive, including among them Mrs Rowlandson and her three

◀ **The Pequot War, 1637, Connecticut. The war was disastrous for the Pequot, who suffered almost total destruction at the hands of the Connecticut militia and allied Indians.**

▲ Settlers of Jamestown, Virginia, engage with Indian attackers in 1607. Note the classic Native American use of cover - the tree trunks would easily stop the settlers' musket balls, even at close range.

children. Eleven weeks of endurance and survival followed, the captives having to keep pace with the fleet-footed warriors, who were hiding from colonial troops during King Philip's War (1675–76), a war between the British Massachusetts settlers and the indigenous tribes. Mary and her two surviving children (her youngest died during the ordeal) were finally ransomed, and some years later she put pen to paper and recounted her ordeal in *A Narrative of the Captivity and Restoration of Mrs. Mary Rowlandson.*

When the book was finally published in 1682 it was an page-turning success, going through four editions in one year alone. Like many similar 'captivity narratives', and colonial accounts of battles with the Native Americans, the Indians were often painted in the most brutal hues. Leaning, like many of the colonists, on

'IT WAS A SOLEMN SIGHT TO SEE SO MANY CHRISTIANS LYING IN THEIR BLOOD, SOME HERE AND SOME THERE, LIKE A COMPANY OF SHEEP TORN BY WOLVES. ALL OF THEM STRIPPED NAKED BY A COMPANY OF HELL-HOUNDS, ROARING, SINGING, RANTING, AND INSULTING, AS IF THEY WOULD HAVE TORN OUR VERY HEARTS OUT.'

her strong Christian faith, Mary decried the Indians as instruments of Satan, seeing them as hellish figures preying on the innocent (see quotation left). It is difficult to see how Rowlandson's judgement on the Indians could fall any lower. Such perceptions of the Native Americans present a problem for any historical study of Indian warfare. The problem is not that the accounts of Indian brutality are necessarily inaccurate, although there are plenty of narratives given to wild exaggeration. Native American tribes could indeed behave with stunning lack of mercy, killing men, women and children with little compunction, and indulging in agonizingly prolonged torture ceremonies centred around unfortunate captives. Rather, the distortion provided by colonial stories is that they frequently present the Native Americans as simple 'savages', their ways of war reduced to little more than barbarism. In an 1835 edition of the British journal *The Monthly Review*, the critic analyses John T. Irving's book *Indian Sketches*, and holds a restrained distaste for the Indians' martial qualities and abilities:

'The author devotes a considerable portion of his work to the delineations of Indian life and exploits, in which the bloodthirsty propensities of these savages are fearfully displayed. The Pawnees, for instance, exhibit a strange mixture of generosity, valour, and cowardice. To steal like an assassin upon an unarmed enemy, and butcher him without the slightest chance of resistance, is a feature in their warfare. In such a case, blood is what is desired, no matter whether from the veins of man, woman, infancy, or age.'

– Monthly Review (1835)

Although the author acknowledges the 'generosity' and 'valour' of the Indians, it is rather the notion of the cowardly assassin, savage murderer of women and children, that comes to the fore. Peoples of the European tradition of warfare generally regarded any sort of covert or self-preserving warfare as ignoble, hence the Native American tactics are generally misinterpreted as either ugly savagery or skulking cowardice.

Such impressions persisted a long way into the twentieth century, perpetuated by Hollywood films and television series. Yet as this book hopes to demonstrate, viewing Native American warfare as savagery overlooks both the subtlety and ingenuity of Indian fighting techniques, and ignores the differences between the Indian situation and the New World being built by the settlers. As we shall see, brutality was the context in which inter-tribal and Indian–settler wars took place – the Native Americans were not the only ones capable of inflicting unnecessary horrors. But that context should not mask the intricacies of a style of warfare that had developed for centuries before the first colonists arrived.

COLONIZATION, DISEASE AND ILLNESS

This book explores the history of the North American warrior from 1500 to the late nineteenth century, encompassing the period in which North America was colonized by Europeans and transformed into the United States and Canada. Some pre-1500 context is required to understand the story fully. The Native Americans had populated parts of North America since at least the tenth century BC, developing their own cultures peculiar to the terrain in which they lived and hunted. Social organization of these peoples revolved around the family, tribes and tribal alliances, with councils and elders acting as simple forms of government. Tribes often conducted trade with one another, bartering both subsistence and luxury goods. Equally, inter-tribal warfare was common, although generally expressed in small-scale raids and clashes, rather than prolonged wars of attrition.

The traditional Indian way of life began an irrevocable change in 1490s, when European colonial powers began their first tentative but purposeful

▲ Meeting of Governor John Carver and Massasoit, chief of the Wampanoag Indians. Massasoit is handing Governor Carver a peace pipe. Meeting with the New Plymouth colonists, the Wampanoag had come dressed and equipped for either peace or war.

explorations of North America. The Spanish and Portuguese pushed up from Central America, while the English and French steadily began colonizing the eastern seaboard of the modern United States and Canada. Europeans brought innovation, ambition and engineering, but to the Indians they also brought disease, suspicion and the belligerent desire to claim the 'New World' as their own. The significance of illness in particular should not be underestimated. Europeans imported diphtheria, cholera, smallpox, influenza, typhus, measles, bubonic plague and a host of other diseases fatal to the indigenous peoples. Entire Native American civilizations were either wiped out or dramatically thinned, leaving the Indians less capable of resisting the depredations to come. Under the umbrella of a 'civilizing mission', the settlers

began their steady programme of expansion, leading to warfare between the Indians and the settlers as the two cultures collided.

THE NATIVE AMERICAN WAY OF WAR

This book explores how the Native American warriors fought both among themselves and against the settlers. Some general principles of Native American warfare are important foundations for subsequent analysis. First, a critical point is that for the Native American, being a warrior was merely one role among others, not a full-time career. As well as being an occasional fighter, the Indian male was also a provider, engaging in trade and hunting for his family and tribe. Self-preservation, therefore, was to a certain degree an obligation, not a choice, and although Indian warriors could be conspicuously or even recklessly brave, most did not value pointless self-sacrifice on the battlefield. This perspective goes a long way towards explaining the attack-and-retreat tactics followed by many Native American tribes, tactics that were regarded with misunderstanding and contempt by the colonists. One early English settler wrote of the local Virginian Indians that they 'were not acquainted with books of military Discipline, that observed no regular Order, that understand not the Souldier's Postures, and Motions, and Firings, and Forms of Battel, that

◀ The coloured areas here reflect typical divisions of the Native American culture areas. The regions represent tremendous geographical diversity, from the woodlands of the east through to the barren tundra of the subarctic far north and the aquatic lifestyles of the Pacific coast.

▲ Iroquois Indians, c.1900. On the left is chief White Head, holding a war dancing stick in his right hand, while in the other, he displays his tobacco pipe and pouch. The headdress is of eagle features.

fight in a base, cowardly, contemptible way.' The writer failed to understand that the Indians were working from entirely different traditions of combat and honour.

A second important point is that Native American warfare was to a large degree derived from traditional hunting skills. The use of ambush and cover, the splitting-up of a war party (misinterpreted by the Europeans as individualism), attacking silently at dawn, the application of camouflage and soft-soled moccasins to deaden footfalls – all such tactics proceeded naturally from the practices of stalking, surprising and trapping a variety of prey. Such skills are extremely hard won and have ready (and sensible) applications in warfare, so it is hardly surprising that the Native Americans were in no rush to adopt

European tactical models, with their general emphasis on open confrontation.

Opening up this analysis, we should also acknowledge that the Indian concept of war in general could be significantly different to that of the Europeans. Native American warfare was born not from combat against European armies, but amongst Indian tribes, which had very different motivations for the prosecution of conflict. Colin F. Taylor, in his recommended book *Native American Hunting and Fighting Skills*, notes that 'the "classic" concept of war – defeat of the people and an imposition of the will of the victor on the losers – was largely alien to the Native Americans' (Taylor, 2003).

He goes on to explain how the Native Americans were rarely ever focused on annihilating an enemy completely, instead 'the underlying ethos of Native American militarism related more to revenge, honor, counting coup, acquiring horses, stealing property and taking prisoners' (Taylor, 2003). These more limited traditions of warfare, which were less socially destructive than the European tradition of 'total war', meant that many Native American war parties would attack, inflict casualties, but then withdraw and not follow up their victory. In this way their military efforts typically had limited horizons, whereas the efforts of the Europeans had complete focus – annihilate or dominate the Indians, and take over their land.

All this being said, the Native Americans were still capable of fielding large armies in times of crisis, not just raiding units and war parties. Forces of up to 2000 warriors, for example, could be mustered by the Timucua and Saturioua tribes of Florida, and warrior groups approaching 1000 men strong were not uncommon in other parts of North America. Yet as history tells us, their numbers were simply insufficient. As time went on, and the settler versus Indian wars became increasingly bitter and macabre, the Native Americans sought to use every tool available to resist the encroachment of the immigrants and their offspring. That they failed to do so is testimony more to the rapacious power of the settlers than the martial skill of the Native Americans.

CHAPTER 1

East Coast Tribes

The tribes of eastern North America occupied a vast swathe of territory, running from the subarctic shores of Canada down to the tropical swamplands of Florida. Although this chapter incorporates the whole eastern slice of North America, in terms of the Native American tribes living there, historians have traditionally divided the territory into two cultural portions – Northeast and Southeast – while also bracketing many of the Eastern tribes as 'Woodlands Indians'.

The 'Woodlands' definition is useful, because it alludes to the fact that the society, warmaking and culture of the Eastern Native American tribes was largely defined by the extremely fertile terrain that dominates the eastern United States and Canada. The Southeast culture area, reaching from the Gulf of Mexico up to the Midwest and out to mid-Texas, was geophysically defined by marshland (saltwater and freshwater), swamps, floodplains (particularly along the mighty Mississippi River), grasslands and the fertile mountains of the southern Appalachians. The Northeast culture area, running from southeastern Canada down to Maryland and Virginia, by contrast, was dominated by

◀ **The battle of Tippecanoe, 7 November 1811. The warriors of Shawnee chief Tecumseh were pitted against a 1000-strong settler force under General William Henry Harrison. Although the Indians launched a stealthy opening attack, they were finally undone by a mass bayonet charge by the militia, a tactic the Indians were unused to facing.**

major river and broadleaf and coniferous forest systems, with elevated land provided by the northern Appalachians. The Great Lakes, and the river systems of the region, provided fishing and trade.

The nature of the terrain in eastern North America was critical in dictating the tactics, weaponry and strategies of the Eastern Native American tribes. As we shall see, in such environments, stealth, ambush and raiding tactics were at a premium, with the Indians essentially practising 'irregular warfare' against the largely conventional tactics of the European settlers.

NORTH AND SOUTH

This study will begin by examining the tribes who inhabited the east, and how they related to one another and to the settlers who colonized their lands. Taking the Northeast area first, the tribes of this territory are often broadly categorized according to their language group – Algonquian-speaking and Iroquois-speaking – although there were some tribes that fell outside of this neat division.

The Iroquois

The Iroquois are particularly interesting for our study, because when they perceived a threat from rival tribes in the late 1500s, they formed a powerful confederacy from the union of five tribes – the Seneca, Oneida, Mohawk, Cayuga and Onondaga –

IROQUOIS FIVE NATIONS TERRITORY 1650

The map here shows the boundaries of the Five Nations of Iroquois in 1650, while the arrows indicate the routes of expansion the tribes took before being curtailed by settler outgrowth. The Iroquois Confederacy was one of the most substantial of the Native American alliances, and it benefited as much from intelligent associations with the colonists as from alliances with one another. The Confederacy was shattered at the end of the eighteenth century, when the Iroquois backing of the British in the American Revolution consigned them to the losing side in the war.

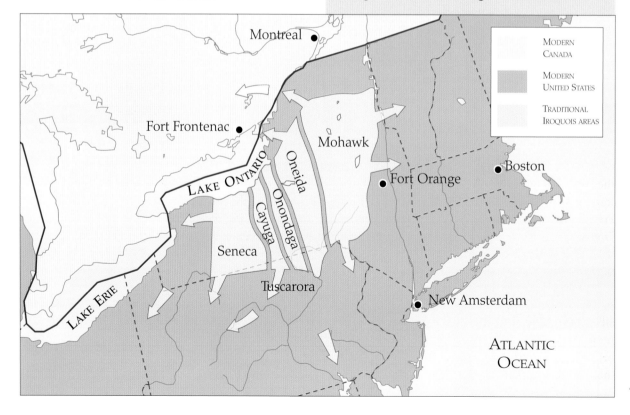

▲ **The northeastern American landscape provided the perfect terrain for Eastern Indian-style warfare. Lakes, rivers and forest trails provided routes of travel, while woodlands gave numerous sites for ambushes.**

with the Tuscarora tribe of North Carolina later joining the Confederacy in the early 1700s (see map on opposite page).

The Iroquois Confederacy was one of the most powerful unified bodies of Native Americans in the whole of North America. Although the confederate structure did not interfere in the individual management of tribal affairs, except in dispute mediation, a 50-member council drawn from all the tribes acted as a kind of 'foreign office' for looking after the Confederacy's interests. The Iroquois increased their power through a close trading relationship with the Dutch and then the British from the early 1600s, associations that brought them imported European firearms. But relations with the French were far less amicable, particularly once French forces allied themselves with the rival Huron tribe in a military campaign against the Iroquois in the Saint Lawrence Valley (see Chapter 2).

The Iroquois' enmity towards the French resulted in frequent attacks on French settlements and an alliance with the British during the French and Indian War (1754–63). The alliance with the British brought the Royal Proclamation of 1763, in which the British guaranteed that all land west of the Appalachians would remain in the hands of the

Native Americans. Iroquois territory, centred in the 1600s to the east and south of Lake Ontario, subsequently expanded south down the Allegheny, Susquehanna and Delaware rivers, east across the Hudson River and west towards Lake Huron. The Iroquois appeared to be in the ascendant.

Yet history had other ideas. Despite four of the six Iroquois nations allying themselves with the British during the American Revolution (1775–83), the British lost their rebellious colony and the Iroquois equally lost significant portions of their land, with many of their peoples heading north into Canada. Those that remained were progressively driven out by an American expansion during the first half of the nineteenth century.

IROQUOIS LOYALIST
An Iroquois warrior shows typical dress for the eighteenth century. Armed with a flintlock 'trade gun', he wears a fabric smock, buckskin leggings (tied with garters to reduce snagging when moving through undergrowth) and has a shaven head decorated with a simple feathered headdress.

THE FRENCH AND INDIAN WAR (1754–63)

This war was principally a war between colonizers – the British and the French – but it inevitably sucked in the Native Americans of the affected territories. The conflict was sparked by the friction between the British and the French in eastern Canada and what would become the northeastern United States. British expansion into Pennsylvania, New York and Ohio Country in the mid-eighteenth century not only displaced many Indian peoples, such as the Delaware and Shawnee, but it also threatened French commercial interests in the Ohio Valley and around the Great Lakes region. Trade relations between the settlers and the Native Americans were disrupted, with some tribes opting to break their associations with the French and form new ties with the British, while others attempted to strike the best deal between the competing Europeans.

By 1753, the French chose to protect their interests by constructing a series of forts from the Great Lakes to the Upper Ohio Valley. The British response consisted of a military expedition led by George Washington, supported by small numbers of Seneca, a campaign that spiralled out of control and led to a major British defeat at Fort Necessity on 4 July 1754, the French having bolstered their forces with Delaware, Ottawa, Algonquin, Wynadot

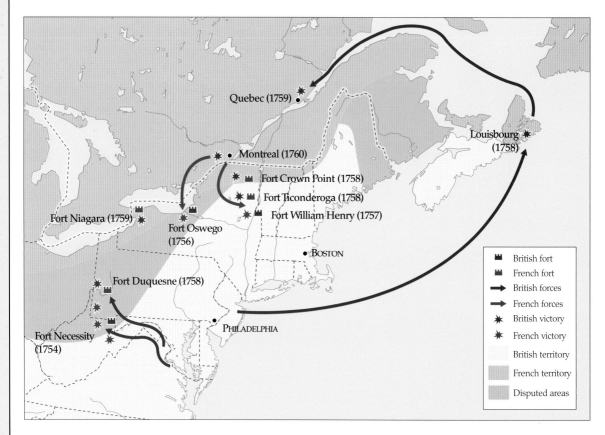

▲ The French and Indian War saw major battles fought between the French and British across the American northwest. Being conducted across traditional Indian lands, the war was as significant for the Native Americans as the European powers.

▲ **The massacre of British settlers, defeated by the French at Fort William Henry in August 1757, was a notorious episode. The French general, Marquis de Montcalm, tried to restrain his allies, but they killed up to 200 settlers, including children.**

and Abenaki allies. So began seven years of conflict as the two powers, plus their Indian allies, struggled for supremacy.

From 1754–58, the French were largely the dominant force in the war, the British suffering major defeats at Fort Oswego (1756) and Fort William Henry (1757). Many Native Americans supported the French, inspired by their apparent ascendancy, and gained a brutal reputation – their massacre of civilians at Fort Oswego brought the lasting antipathy of many British settlers. British attempts to recruit their own Indian allies had mixed results: poor handling of Cherokee allies, for example, resulted in an Anglo–Cherokee War 1759–61. Yet in the late 1750s, the British started

to send reinforcements and better commanders, and make firmer alliances with Iroquois tribes. From the autumn of 1758 until 1760, the French suffered a string of critical defeats, culminating in the losses of Quebec and Montreal. In 1763, the Treaty of Paris saw the French concede almost all their North American territories to the British. Indian tribes also suffered consequent loss of territory, and the Iroquois in particular lost their influence as intermediaries between the Europeans.

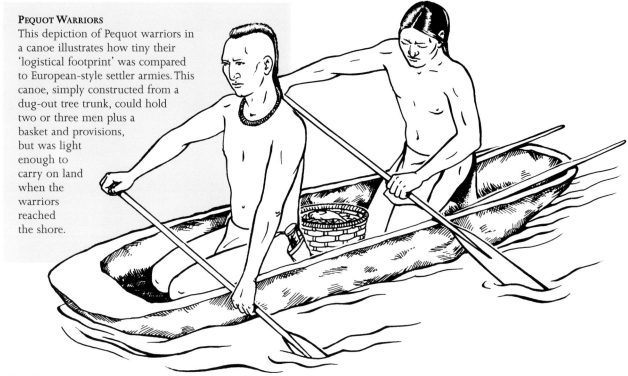

PEQUOT WARRIORS
This depiction of Pequot warriors in a canoe illustrates how tiny their 'logistical footprint' was compared to European-style settler armies. This canoe, simply constructed from a dug-out tree trunk, could hold two or three men plus a basket and provisions, but was light enough to carry on land when the warriors reached the shore.

The Algonquian

The Algonquian-speaking nations also formed various confederacies, although with looser structures than that employed by the Iroquois. The less rigid organization was somewhat natural given the large numbers of Algonquian tribes, which included the Abenaki, Delaware, Mohegan, Narragansett, Pequot, Nanticoke, Algonquin and Shawnee. Like the Iroquois, the Algonquian confederacies had to adjust to the realities of colonial expansion during the seventeenth century, meeting them with a mix of compromise and military resistance. The fate of one of the alliances,

the Powhatan Confederacy, is typical. Named after Chief Powhatan (this is his anglicized name – his real name was Wahunsunacock), the Powhatan Confederacy was formed at the beginning of the seventeenth century in Virginia and grew to a strength of 30 tribes. It has the dubious honour of being among the first Native American cultures to encounter the colonizing British, who put down permanent roots in Virginia in 1607 around Jamestown. In his 1781–82 work *Notes on the State of Virginia*, Thomas Jefferson noted in around 1607:

'THE TERRITORIES OF THE POWHATAN CONFEDERACY, SOUTH OF THE PATOWMAC, COMPREHENDED ABOUT 8000 SQUARE MILES [20,720 SQUARE KM], 30 TRIBES, AND 2400 WARRIORS. CAPT. SMITH TELLS US, THAT WITHIN 60 MILES [96KM] OF JAMES TOWN WERE 5000 PEOPLE, OF WHOM 1500 WERE WARRIORS. FROM THIS WE FIND THE PROPORTION OF THEIR WARRIORS TO THEIR WHOLE INHABITANTS, WAS AS 3 TO 10. THE POWHATAN CONFEDERACY THEN WOULD CONSIST OF ABOUT 8000 INHABITANTS, WHICH WAS ONE FOR EVERY SQUARE MILE [2.5 SQUARE KM]; BEING ABOUT THE TWENTIETH PART OF OUR PRESENT POPULATION IN THE SAME TERRITORY, AND THE HUNDREDTH OF THAT OF THE BRITISH ISLANDS.'

CHIEF POWHATAN

Known more properly as Wahunsunacock, Powhatan (c.1548–1618) was one of the great historical leaders of the Algonquian Indians. Powhatan was something of an opportunist – he initially negotiated and dealt with the British settlement around Jamestown, and was known to provide food to them on some occasions. He also made profitable alliances with the British to assist in his wars against other Indian tribes. Yet conversely, he saw that the settlers were intent on acquiring more land, which led to his formation of the Powhatan Confederacy. He launched several raids against the colonists but in 1614 his daughter, Pocahontas, married an English settler, John Rolfe, and for the next four years until his death in 1618 he was at peace with the British.

▼ **An idealized image of Chief Powhatan communicating with the settlers. Here, he meets John Rolfe, who would marry his daughter, Pocahontas.**

CHEROKEE IN TRADITIONAL OUTFIT
A Cherokee male shows a mixture of functional and ceremonial items of dress, including a buckskin jacket with criss-crossing ornamental sash, a blanket or robe over one shoulder and soft moccasin shoes.

The evident strength of the Powhatan Confederacy enabled it to resist British attempts at subduing it, take on the Spaniards and also drive the rival Chesapeake tribe to destruction. Yet it was largely the great Powhatan himself who held the Confederacy together. By the time he died in 1618, he had established reasonably peaceful relations with the British settlers, but his efforts were utterly undone by his successor, his half-brother Opechancanough. Legitimately fearing British expansion, in March 1622 Opechancanough launched a massive strike against the British, killing nearly 350 colonists. Yet he had not counted on the European military response, and between 1622 and 1646 the British and the Powhatans found themselves locked in regular war. Using their superior firepower, the British forces inflicted a steadily mounting toll upon the Indian tribes, although another major Indian attack on 18 April 1644 resulted in the death of a further 500 colonists. The British response was vigorous and violent, and by the spring of 1646, Opechancanough was captured

▲ Captain John Smith taking Chief Opechancanough, war leader of the Pamunkey tribe, prisoner in 1646. Opechancanough was a major force in the Powhatan Wars and, after his capture, was murdered by a settler, angered by Opechancanough's 'insurgency'.

and killed and large tracts of Algonquian land placed under British rule. The Powhatan Confederacy lasted only another four or five years before it finally broke part and its peoples dispersed.

The Southeast

In the Southeast culture area, there were more than 50 tribes at the time in contact with the colonial settlers. These tribes included the Alabama, Catawba, Cherokee, Chickasaw, Choctaw, Creek, Natchez and Seminole. The Cherokee are a particularly famous and interesting example of Native American warmaking. Spread across a wide region, from Virginia down to Georgia, the Cherokees were a generally independent collection of towns and villages until war threatened, when dedicated war chiefs would coordinate all the towns' efforts. The Cherokee first clashed with the settlers in 1654 when the Virginia Cherokee suffered a heavy defeat at the hands of settler infantry backed by Pamunkey Indians. Over the next 100 years, relations between the Cherokees and the colonists deteriorated into a state of regular war, culminating in the Cherokee War of 1759–61, which resulted in the tribe losing large parts of their territory in South and North Carolina to the British.

From the 1760s to the mid-1790s, the Cherokee were split into factions, some advocating peace with the settlers, while others prosecuted an insurgency against them. Yet in 1794, those resisting were largely defeated and Cherokee warriors even became auxiliary troops for American forces. Bad times were not over, however, and in 1835 the signing of the New Echota Treaty led to the expulsion of the Cherokee from their ancestral lands to the new Indian Territory in Oklahoma. The subsequent traumatic journey there became known as the Trail of Tears. The remainder of the nineteenth century saw the Cherokee torn apart by internal disputes, increased by wavering loyalties during the American Civil War, and the final story was largely one of dispossession. The story of the Cherokee was not unusual amongst the Native American tribes of the nineteenth century. Yet the overriding narrative of eventual defeat should not mask some of the impressive realities of the Native Americans in combat.

TRAIL OF TEARS Early 1800s

The trail of tears was an infamous act of inhumanity by the settlers towards the Native Americans. The Indian Removal Act of 1830 pushed Southeastern tribes from their centuries-old homelands out to new territories in the west. The displacement was often performed under military duress, and thousands died in transit or in harshly run settlements.

Missouri
Illinois
Kentucky
Oklahoma
North Carolina
South Carolina
Arkansas
Mississippi
Alabama
Georgia
Texas
Florida
Louisiana

RESERVATIONS

CHEROKEE HOMELANDS

WEAPONS

Before we study the actual warfighting tactics of the Eastern Indians, we must first appreciate the tools with which they fought. The most basic fighting weapon in terms of construction was the war club. There were several different styles. One

▲ **This warclub may have been intended for ceremonial purposes, on account of the decorated impact head. This club is of the older, ball-headed type, as opposed to the gunstock type often seen after settler contact.**

featured a rounded ball-like head as the striking point, the head set forward of the haft. French clergyman Joseph Francois Lafitau (1681–1746) described it as 'made of a tree root, or some other very hard wood, two or two and a half feet long [0.6–0.75m], squared on the sides, and widened or rounded to the width of a fist at its end' (quoted in Jones, 2004). An extant club from Massachusetts, dating back to the seventeenth century, was made

from the ball root of a maple tree, and was elaborately decorated with white and purple *wampum* (*wampum* is bead decoration made from shells, typically those of whelks or clams). Other Eastern Indian club weapons more resembled wooden swords, with sharpened edges providing something of a cutting effect, or were fitted with antler, stone, bone or metal spikes to create a penetrating injury. Later clubs, known as gunstock clubs, were shaped in a similar fashion to a musket stock, with the addition of a metal blade to provide a cutting effect.

The Tomahawk

Related to the club was the tomahawk, today regarded as a defining weapon of the native Americans. The tomahawk is closely related to the Eastern Indians, the word coming from the Algonquian *otomahuk*, meaning 'to strike down'. At first, tomahawk heads were made from nothing more than shaped rock or a piece of soapstone, or a large section of bone, fastened to a haft measuring approximately 0.6m (2ft) in length. The haft itself was made of a local wood such as hickory, maple or ash.

◀ **Two examples of pipe tomahawks, one with a conventional axe blade (bottom), the other featuring a pick-type weapon. The introduction of steel by the settlers improved the tomahawk as a durable weapon.**

THROWING A TOMAHAWK
Throwing a tomahawk
required long hours of
practice to perfect. For a
distance of about 3m
(12ft), the thrower
aimed to make the
tomahawk describe
one full revolution
before striking the
target, blade first.
The more wrist
flick applied, the
faster the axe spun
in the air, while a
looser wrist
slowed the spin.

Pipe tomahawks were made for ceremonial purposes by carving a pipe bowl into the poll of the axe, the smoke being drawn down the hollowed-out handle.

The effectiveness of the tomahawk was dramatically improved with the adoption of iron heads, which increased the weight, sharpness and durability of the blade. Such qualities were important, as the tomahawk was as much used for utility purposes, such as chopping wood and meat, as it was for combat. During a fight, however, the tomahawk was often thrown as well as being used hand-to-hand. A striking picture of the lethality of the tomahawk comes from an edition of the *New Monthly Magazine*, a collection of stories published in 1827. In an article entitled 'A Canadian Campaign, by a British Officer', a British soldier recounts a major expedition against Indian tribes in the southeastern United States, and explains the following encounter:

'In this affair, I had an opportunity of particularly witnessing the cruel dexterity and despatch with which the Indians use the tomahawk and scalping-knife. An American rifleman who had been dismounted within a few paces of the spot where I stood, was fired at by three warriors of the Delaware tribe. The unfortunate man received the several balls in his body, yet, though faint and tottering from loss of blood, he made every exertion to save himself. The foremost of his pursuers was a tall powerful man. When arrived within fifteen paces of his victim, uncovered in his flight, he threw his tomahawk, and with such force and precision, that it immediately opened the skull and extended him motionless on the earth. Laying down his rifle, he drew forth his knife, and after having removed the hatchet from the brain, proceeded to make a circular incision throughout the scalp. This done, he grasped the bloody instrument between his teeth, and placing his knees on the back of his victim, while at the same time he fastened his hands in the hair, the scalp was torn off without much apparent difficulty, and thrust still bleeding into his bosom. The warrior then arose, and after having wiped his knife on the clothes of the unhappy man, returned it to its sheath, grasping at the same time the arms he had abandoned, and hastening to rejoin his comrades. All this was the work of a minute.'

This episode clearly illustrates the power of the tomahawk, as evidenced by its ability to bury itself into a man's skull. We also gain an insight into the terrible practice of scalping, about which more will be said in later chapters. Skill with the tomahawk, however, took a long period of time to develop, as the hunter required a rapid and intuitive understanding of how many turns the tomahawk would make in flight so that it struck with the blade and not with another part of the weapon. Furthermore, if the tomahawk was his primary weapon, the Indian would find himself virtually defenceless once it had been thrown, hence in combat situations he was often more likely to use it as a hand-held weapon, taking advantage of its superiority when compared with the knife.

Daggers

By the eighteenth century, the Eastern Native Americans were increasingly using metal daggers as weapons of war. Prior to the arrival of the colonists, Indian blades were made largely of bone or rock, the latter 'pressure-flaked' with the edge of an antler to form a rudimentary but

dangerous blade. Some copper blades were manufactured, but with the arrival of the settlers the Indians began to purchase far more durable iron blades. A particularly popular style of knife was the 'beaver tail' blade that, as its name suggests, had a broad double-edged blade tapering to an efficient point. The Indians developed gaudy sheaths to go with their blades, often encompassing hilt as well as blade, possibly suggesting that the knives were used more for utility and hunting than as a rapid-response weapon in combat. The Indians also made their own knives by sharpening up pieces of scrap metal and wrapping the 'tang' (handle) with strips of hide to form a basic hilt.

Bows

Spears were common Indian weapons, at least up to around 1650, used for both fishing and hunting game. From the late seventeenth century onwards, however, spears were largely replaced for land hunting and warfare with firearms, although their practicality for fishing meant that their use did not die out altogether. Furthermore, Native American thrusting spears made poor weapons when compared to the metal-headed spears and pole arms brought into North America by the colonizing Europeans.

When faced by these, and the settlers' firearms, the bow and arrow made a far more equalizing weapons system. The exact type of bow used by Native

SCALPING

Scalping was one of the most notorious of Native American practices. The act could involve cutting away portions of skin, from a small disk of flesh around the crown of the skull, to the entire top portion of scalp, running from ear to ear. The scalps were retained as decorative, symbolic and ceremonial items, signifying the warrior's bravery.

▲ Native American warriors attacking an early seventeenth-century family of European settlers. Such depictions increased the hostility between white colonists and the Indian tribes living around the new settlements.

ARCHERS
The Eastern tribes used self-bows made from hickory, ash or locust wood. A typical length was about 170cm (67in) and arrows were tipped with either flint, bone or steel heads. The bow was accompanied by an arrow quiver, made from hide and often decorated with tassels.

Americans varied according to the tribe, available materials and the nature of the territory, but for the Eastern Indians, the most common type was the self-bow, meaning that the bow was made of a single piece of wood without the addition of pieces of sinew, horn or bone.

Surrounded by plentiful supplies of high-quality woods, the Woodland Indians made a natural choice in their preference for self-bows, despite the fact that these traditionally have less power and range than composite or sinew-backed bows. Colin Taylor observes that there 'is little question that the Woodland bow lacked the power of the traditional English longbow, with the Indian bow having of pull of up to 23kg (50lb), while the longbow pull could climb well beyond 32kg (70lb)' (Taylor, 2003).

Yet Taylor goes on to point out that the pull comparison is largely a paper exercise and that the difference in power lost much of its relevance in battle:

'Subsequent events, however, demonstrated that it [the Woodland bow] could have deadly effect at close range and in the hands of a skilled warrior. In 1636, when the Pequot killed several of Lion Gardiner's men at Fort Saybrook, Gardiner reported that "the body of one man shot through, the arrow going in at the right side, the head sticking fast, half through a rib on the left side." He sent both the arrow and the man's rib to officials in Massachusetts Bay Colony "because they had said the arrows of the Indians were of no force."'

– *Taylor* (2003)

Spears
These varied hugely in construction from simple sticks, sharpened with the point hardened over a

fire, to carefully crafted missiles featuring flights and a separate flint spearhead bound onto the shaft by animal sinews. As this distinction suggests, Indian spears were broadly separated into two different categories – stabbing spears and throwing spears. The former were generally used to finish off injured game, while the latter served as a ranged weapon against dangerous animals, or enemies. The range and penetration of a throwing spear could be increased by the use of the atlatl, a spear-throwing device. This was essentially a hooked stick about 45cm (18in) long into which the heel of the spear was slotted. By throwing the spear forwards using the atlatl, the user could increase the acceleration applied to it, and hence improve its distance and power. However, the space required to use the atlatl effectively meant that it was less popular among the Eastern territories, with its dense woodlands, than it was further out west and in the subarctic north, where open spaces and large prey such as buffalo meant the spear thrower could be used to its full potential (see Chapter 3).

▲ **A settler engraving shows Native American youths shooting arrows and throwing balls at targets and engaging in running races. Athleticism and warrior skills were taught from infancy.**

As discussed, the Woodland bow had plenty of power within its effective range. Its penetration was further enhanced by the quality of its arrows. The arrow shafts themselves were made from canes or bones, smoothed out with a knife or scraper to remove any imperfections. Arrowheads were crafted from a variety of materials, such as shards of stone, flint or

SPEAR POINTS
A collection of flint arrowheads from the Eastern Woodlands, dating back to prehistoric times. Some arrowheads were loosely attached to the arrow shaft, causing them to detach inside prey and produce more serious injuries over time.

bone, or pieces of shell, wood, horn or antler. The arrowhead would be set in a split at the end of the shaft, and lashed into place with sinew, rawhide or plant material. However, sometimes the head would be set loose in the shaft so that it would detach in a prey or enemy to increase the complications, hence the severity, of the wound.

Practical combat range in the confined woods and forests of the Eastern territories did not require a bow that could shoot out to hundreds of metres. Woodland warriors attempted to close the distance between themselves and their enemy as much as possible before taking the shot – this mirrored how they practised hunting. In addition, after a lifetime of practice they could deliver the arrows to the target with astonishing accuracy. Daniel Harman, a partner in the North West Company in 1808, explained how the Cree Indians, whose territories butted up against the eastern regions, began honing their bow skills from infancy:

'Their youth, from the age of four or five to that of eighteen or twenty years, pass nearly half of their time in shooting arrows at a mark ... From so early and constant a practice, they become, at length, the best marksmen, perhaps, in the world. Many of them, at a

distance of eight or ten rods [a rod is equivalent to 5m/16ft 6in], will throw an arrow with such precision, as twice out of three times, to hit a mark the size of a dollar.'

– Daniel Harman (1808)

Firearms

In addition to accuracy, it could be argued that for a significant period of time, arguably from 1500 until the nineteenth century, bows actually delivered superior firepower when compared to the muzzle-loading firearms of the time. A flintlock musket, even in well-trained hands, was only capable of around two or three aimed shots every minute, less once the gun had become fouled during battle. The bow, however, could shoot an arrow every 10 seconds and had no problems with fouling, damp powder or an imperfect flint. The only drawback of the bow when compared to the musket was that the former took years of practice to perfect, whereas a few weeks' instruction with a firearm would bring enough practical, if not expert, proficiency.

Of course, in time, guns would change everything for the Eastern Indians as for the other Native Americans of the United States. The Eastern Indians were the first to encounter firearms, and were undoubtedly impressed by their flash and thunder, if not by their performance. On 29 July 1609, the French explorer Samuel de Champlain, along with a party of a few Europeans and about 60 allied Native American warriors, were confronted by a war party of about 200 Iroquois or Mohawks. De Champlain loaded four

ATLATL THROWING TECHNIQUE
The atlatl was a simple device for increasing the acceleration behind a spear throw. Note how the warrior first uses the momentum of a run, then a deep lunge, to apply his full body weight to the throw. The whipping action of the atlatl greatly amplifies this force.

▲ **An Indian Wars re-enactor shows a typical flintlock firearm. The Eastern Indians found flintlock firearms more practical than the Plains Indians, as they mostly fought on foot rather than horseback.**

balls into his matchlock arquebus and fired at his opponents – the single shot killed two enemy chiefs and wounded another man. Such was the surprise that the war party retreated and dispersed.

Once the shock of the new had worn off, however, the Eastern Indians began purchasing guns from the settlers. They used these firearms to settle tribal scores, hence the Cree and the Chippewa Indians were able to force the Sioux out from the western regions of the Eastern Woodlands around 1700, and push them towards the plains that would become their homeland. The Mohawk performed similar feats against the Delaware Confederation.

At first, the firearms bought by the Indians were matchlock arquebus types, the powder in the pan detonated by a glowing match. The matchlock mechanism was not suited to hunting – the light and the smell generated by the match gave the user's presence away to sensitive game animals – and its unreliability in damp woodland conditions meant that the bow was still king.

The balance changed slightly in the second half of the seventeenth century, when more reliable flintlock weapons became available to the Indians through British, Dutch and French traders. Ironically, the Native Americans actually proved more skilful in the use of firearms than their suppliers; a lifetime of training in accurate bow shooting translated into generally

excellent musket marksmanship. Later on, by the early nineteenth century, the Indians sought to acquire rifled instead of smoothbore firearms, appreciating the additional range and accuracy of such weapons.

ARMOUR

Although the Native Americans are popularly seen either bare-chested or wearing loose, soft garments, they also had their own armour. Shields, for example, were common pieces of war-fighting kit amongst the Eastern tribes. In the northeast, the shields tended to be fairly plain and unadorned, but they came in a wide spectrum of types.

Some were constructed from a wooden section of willow or similar wood and wrapped with animal skins, while others might consist of nothing more than multiple layers of leather formed into a square shield with a handgrip at the back. The historian David E. Jones explains some of the other varieties found in the northeast:

'The Wampanoag warriors of Cape Cod used shields made of bark slabs (Steel [1994]). The Huron warrior carried one of two types – one a small rawhide shield and the other of bark and almost large enough to cover a man's body. The Miamis' shields were made of buffalo rawhide. Long rawhide shields are reported for the Potawatomi, Illinois and Ottawa (Pritzker [1998], 2). The Lenape in Pennsylvania and Delaware preferred large wooden or moose rawhide shields (ibid).'

– Jones (2004)

IROQUOIS WITH FLINTLOCK MUSKET

An Iroquois warrior stands with a crudely contoured 'trade gun' musket. The Northeastern Indians tended to use firearms modelled more on French types, as the Indians were familiar with these from the early days of European settlement. Note that this warrior wears a small section of slat armour, over the groin area.

A similar wide variety of war shields was seen in the southeastern territories, including wicker shields. Although wicker is itself a fairly insubstantial material, contemporary accounts indicate that in the shields it was so tightly woven that arrows would not penetrate. (Jones notes that the Spanish discovered that even crossbow bolts were unable to punch through the wicker shields.)

In combat, the warrior might grip the shield with his left hand (or vice versa), positioning it to protect his torso while leaving his right hand free to wield a tomahawk or knife. Archers might also hang the shield from one of their shoulders while taking a shot, in so doing protecting an exposed side of the body.

In addition to shields, the Eastern Indians also had numerous varieties of body armour, although the pattern of distribution varies according the region. In the northeast, the armour was typically made of slats or rods of wood, bone, wicker or rawhide, the whole structure sewn together with rawhide and worn as a form of breastplate via a strap around the neck. Alternatively, the armour might be made from a single piece of wood and wrapped in thick material as padding. Separate pieces could be added to the armour to protect the back and the upper portions of the legs. Although little seen in visual records, some literary sources also refer to the Iroquois wearing helmets, produced from hoops of branches or wicker and bound together with twine.

Travelling further south, references to body armour become fewer, although not completely absent. Some illustrations show a gorget worn around the neck, basically a disk of wood, shell, slate or even metal about 25cm (10in) across and hung over the upper chest, although the primary purpose of this device may well have been ceremonial rather than protective.

Prior to the introduction of firearms, the Native American armour and shields would have been capable of stopping most arrows and hand-thrown spears. The introduction of guns, however, changed matters irrevocably. Apart from against the heaviest shields, musket balls fired from later firearms (from the eighteenth century onwards) would typically penetrate a wicker breastplate or buffalo hide shield. In

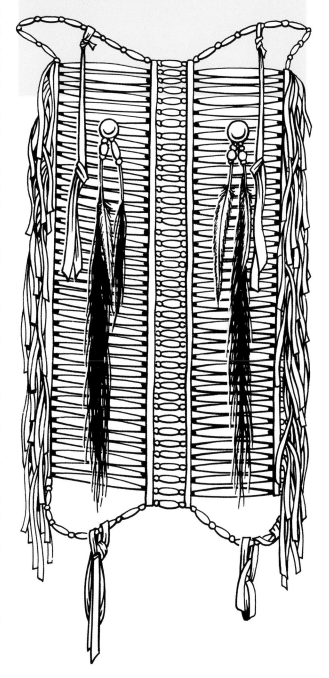

BREASTPLATE
An elaborate armoured breastplate, featuring two sections composed of wooden rods and slats bound tightly together with rawhide cord. Such armour provided decent protection for centuries before the arrival of the settlers. Once the settlers came, however, armour was made increasingly redundant by the penetrative power of firearms.

▲ **An Eastern Canadian Native American dressed in traditional dress, dancing and taking part in a** *pow-wow* **(a council or meeting of Indians). As well as carrying many ceremonial items, he wears a long breastplate of slat armour, which was traditionally made of wood, reed or pieces of bone.**

consequence, armour was largely irrelevant by the nineteenth century, and was relegated to ceremonial usage.

FORTIFICATIONS

Fortifications are a little-appreciated aspect of Native American warfare. The Native Americans were surrounded by a dangerous world, every village and community being threatened by raids or more substantial attacks. In response, the Eastern Native Americans (and others, as we shall see) sometimes fortified their permanent villages or camps, producing edifices of genuine defensive sophistication.

By 1500, the single-wall palisade defence, sometimes with a wet or dry ditch surrounding it, had evolved into fortifications with two, three or four concentric palisades, the palisades formed from thick poles. The palisades could rise 9m (30ft) high, and the ground between them was laid with tree trunks to provide a form of walkway, or were criss-crossed with flexible boughs, bound together at the top with rawhide to form another obstacle to movement, should anyone manage to penetrate the outer defences. Above the palisades rose watchtowers and defensive galleries, used as fighting platforms from which rocks, arrows, missiles and gunfire could be directed at any attacking forces.

Some of the best descriptions of Indian fortifications come from French observers. One of them, Joseph Lafitau, writing in the eighteenth century, provides an excellent and detailed description of an Iroquois outpost:

'The villages most vulnerable to hostile forces are fortified by a palisade 15–20ft [4.5–6m] high, composed of three rows of posts, those in the middle set straight and perpendicular, the others crossing each other at an angle like saw-bucks, reinforced by heavy, dense bark to the height of 10 or 12ft [3–3.5m]. Inside this palisade, the Indians have ordered a kind of gallery or circular walk created by trees laid horizontally, all joining the palisade and set on large forked posts of wood stuck into the ground. At regular intervals, there are redoubts or watch towers, which in times of war are filled up with stones to defend against scaling attacks and for pouring water to put out fire. They [the defenders] climb up there using steps cut into the trunks of trees which act as ladders. The palisade also has openings cut into it to serve as battlements. The nature of the terrain determines the shape of their enclosures. They are sometimes shaped as polygons, but the largest number are round or spherical in shape ...

The palisade has only one exit, via a narrow door set at a slant, closing with a cross bar, through which people have to pass sideways.'

– Lafitau (1724)

The structure of this fortification, as described by Lafitau, must have presented a genuine challenge to any attacker, especially with significant fire coming from the battlements. In fact, often the attacking force would avoid attacking the fortification at all, instead taunting the occupants until some of them ventured

COHOKIA FORT
The Cohokia fort, located near Collinsville, Illinois, is a fine example of early Native American fort building. It featured an extensive outer palisade that wrapped around many of the settlement's habitations. Acting almost like a medieval European bailey was a massive terraced 'mound' capped by a ceremonial temple building. Although the Cohokia Fort lapsed into disuse just before 1500, it illustrates that defensive sophistication was part of Indian culture even before the settlers arrived.

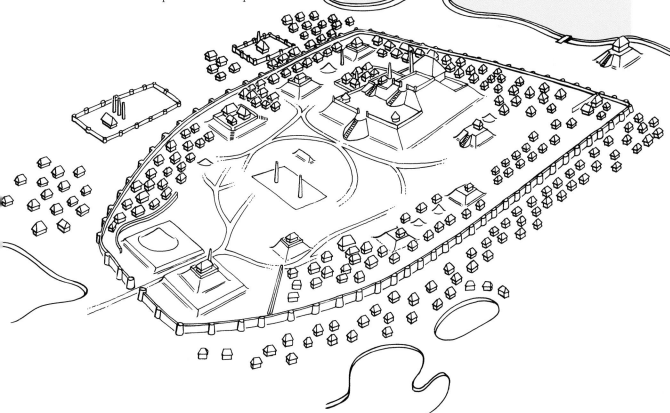

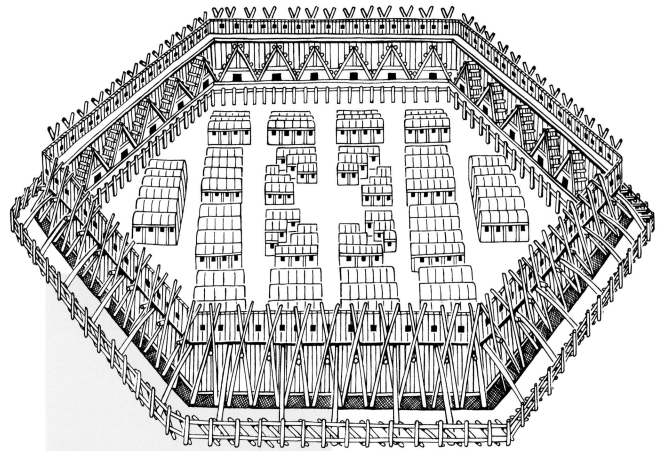

IROQUOIS FORTIFICATION
This diagrammatic representation of an Iroquois
fortification illustrates the sophistication of Native
American defensive design. The outer defences
consist of a low palisade, then a stretch of ground,
broken up by poles, before the main defensive walls.
The stretch of open ground served as a killing area
for the defenders, who fired bows and firearms as
the attackers struggled for entry.

outside and were killed or injured, at which point the
attackers would consider their job done.

Yet although the fortifications were undoubtedly a
fearsome proposition for attack by Indians in the pre-
firearms arm, there were some contemporary
European observers who gave them little value in the
Early Modern age. Writing in 1653, the Dutch New
Netherland landowner, Adriaen Cornelissen van der
Donck, acknowledged the intelligent structural set-up

of the local Northeast Indian fortifications, but draws
a sceptical conclusion:

'In the villages and castles they always do solid and
good work. As sites for their castles they tend to prefer,
if possible, a high or steep hill near water or a
riverside, which is difficult to climb up and often
accessible on one side only. They always take care also
that it is flat and even on top. This they enclose with a
very heavy wooden stockade constructed in a peculiar
interlocking diamond pattern. First they lay a heavy
tree along the ground on both sides, which forms a
cross at the upper end where they are notched to fit
tighter together. Next another tree is laid in there to
make a very solid work. The palisades stand two deep,
sufficiently strong to protect them from a surprise
attack or sudden raid by their enemies, but they do not
as yet have any knowledge of properly equipping such

a work with curtains, bastions, and flanking walls. They also build some small forts here and there on the level and low land near their plantations to shelter their wives and children from an assault, in case they have enemies so nearby that they could be fallen upon by small parties. They think highly of their forts and castles built in that fashion, but these actually are of little consequence, and cause them more harm than good in war with the Christians."

– Snow *et al.* (1996)

Van der Donck highlights the fact that it was not the fortification alone that presented the challenge for the war party; the location of the fortified village would ideally add to its security. Yet his statement at the end that, in effect, the fortifications were strategically pointless should not be taken at face value, and appears to be European condescension. Certainly, the introduction of heavy artillery into American warfare would seem to pose a significant threat to a lashed wooden structure. The work of historian David Jones, however, throws Van der Donck's perspective

into question. He describes how the French around New Orleans, led by Governor Bienville, allied themselves with the Choctaw Indians in an effort to defeat the belligerent Chickasaw tribe.

The first problem that confronted Bienville was that the fortified village of Ackia, his main target, was protected by two other hill forts. This mutually supportive defensive arrangement meant that Bienville had to tackle all three strongpoints at once if he were to avoid his forces being devastated by crossfire or fire to his rear. Furthermore, the Chickasaw shot flaming arrows into flammable outlying structures, the resulting smoke making the French efforts even more

CREEK VILLAGE
This Creek Indian village is protected mainly by an outer forest – Indian scouts and guard dogs would typically alert the occupants to any intruders (particularly heavy-footed settlers) before they even arrived. The Indians occupy wood-framed houses, insulated with foliage, and animal fodder is stored behind in a fenced area. The warrior in the centre carries a matchlock musket.

complicated, resulting in an eventually ineffective attack. Bienville, in an official report back to France, also pointed out that Indians fought from shoulder-high holes dug into the ground, and would cover defensive cabins with 'a wall of earth and wood proof against burning arrows and grenades so that nothing but bombs can harm them' (see Jones [2004]).

Such was the nature of Indian fortifications that the colonists required major artillery resources if they were to attack them in a direct assault. Jones points to an official Ministry of the Colonies letter dated 1 January 1739, which reveals the ordnance required by an attacking army to effectively take on a fortified Chickasaw village:

'As for the artillery, since the Chickasaw villages that are to be attacked are fortified, it was thought advisable to send four eight-pounder cannon; eight four-pounders, six of which carry ammunition for three shots; two nine-pounder mortars of brass; two of iron of six-pound caliber; twelve other small mortars of wrought-iron which were forged for this purpose; and powder, bullets, bombs and the tools necessary to make use of them.'

This list shows that the artillery deemed necessary to take on the Indian village is substantial, indicating that cracking an Indian fort was not casual matter for European colonists, even equipped as they were with the modern engines of war.

Yet despite the evidence that extensive firepower was necessary, and to be fair to Van der Donck's views given earlier, in the grand totality of the campaigns of the Eastern Indians to preserve their native territories, the fortifications did not ultimately succeed. Why this is so will be address in the next section.

◀ A seventeenth-century engraving shows Native American raiders, armed with bows and firearms, setting fire to the town of Deerfield in Franklin County, Massachusetts.

TACTICS

'Indisciplined' Warfare

As already noted in the Introduction, Indian warmaking was very different to that of the European settlers. Typically, colonial interpretations of Indian warfare and tactics emphasized native 'indiscipline', as compared to the ordered ranks and hierarchical structure of European-style armies. Yet history has consistently shown us that the Native American warriors actually possessed discipline in plentiful supply, but just of a different manner. Armstrong Starkey, writer of the study *European and Native American Warfare 1675–1815*, has commented on this different type of martial discipline:

'In contrast to European armies, Indian discipline was founded on individual honour rather than corporal punishment; leaders were chosen according to merit based on courage and experience instead of privilege or purchase. Commanders were concerned to save their men's lives and believed that victory did not justify unnecessary sacrifice. There was no disgrace in retreating to await a more favourable occasion for battle. Indian leaders taught their men to move in scattered order and take advantage of the ground, to surround the enemy or to avoid being surrounded. They practised running and marksmanship and

they became accustomed to endure hunger and hardship with patience and fortitude.'

– Starkey (1998)

Starkey describes a type of discipline and intelligence that would be far more appreciable to modern special forces, rather than the tradition-bound ranks of Revolutionary War European armies.

Looking at the Eastern Native Americans specifically, this instinctive discipline expressed itself in warfare in several ways. First, as Starkey notes, the Native Americans made excellent use of terrain. From their experience of hunting in the woodlands, the Eastern warriors prioritized stealthy deployment of their forces into good ambush positions or places from which a sudden attack could be launched. In essence, they followed modern procedures of cover and concealment by using hills, depressions, rivers, dense foliage and other

WOODLAND ARCHER
This simply dressed Eastern Indian takes up an ambush position. Note how he grips an arrow in each hand to facilitate quick reloading – a trained warrior would be able to fire an aimed shot every seven or eight seconds. As a back-up weapon, he wears a dagger on his waist, the blade probably purchased from the settlers.

AMBUSH
A group of Native American raiders move into ambush position overlooking a colonial settlement and its valuable livestock. They take advantage of the settlement's outer perimeter fence to conceal their movements. The warriors might wait in this position for hours, withholding their attack until the first light of dawn or an opportunity for surprise.

natural features to stay out of sight until the moment to attack came. Moreover, the war party would often move through this terrain in loose order (another reason why the Europeans interpreted them as indisciplined), each man taking his own route while being instinctively aware of the others around him. As with hunting, the war party members would try to manoeuvre themselves so that the enemy (the prey) were trapped and had no easy route of escape. Often one group would act as a primary attacking force, while another set up an ambush position along the enemy's line of retreat to hit them as they fell back.

The experience for the victims of an Indian ambush could be disconcerting to say the least. Daniel Gookin (1612–87), a settler who lived in Virginia and

Massachusetts and wrote extensively on the Native Americans and their practices, explained how actually fighting against the Indians quickly cured the settlers of any misconceptions:

'But it was found another manner of thing than expected; for our man could see no enemy to shoot at, but yet felt their bullets out of the thick bushes where they lay in ambushments. The enemy also used this strategem, to apparel themselves from the waist upwards with green boughs, that our Englishman could not readily discern them from the natural bushes; this manner of fighting our men had little experience of, and hence they were under great disadvantage.'

Gookin's quotation highlights the fact that the Woodland Indians were also masters of camouflage, using green leafy bows or animal skills to blend in with their terrain, and break up their silhouettes to enemy musketeers. A nineteenth-century account of a Virginia rifleman on guard duty on the Plains of

Chippewa during the French and Indian War speaks of the audacity with which the Eastern Native American could apply his camouflage skills:

'At length, a low rustling among the bushes on the right caught his ear. He gazed long towards the spot whence the sound seemed to proceed, but saw nothing, save the impenetrable gloom of the thick forest which surrounded the encampment. Then, as he marched onward, he heard o'er the gentle breeze of night, the joyful cry of 'all's well', after which, he seated himself upon a stump, and dropped in a deep fit of musing. While he thus sat, a Savage entered the open space behind him, and, after buckling his tunic, with its numerous folds, tight around his body, drew over his head the skin of a wild boar, with the natural appendages of these animals; and, thus accoutred, walked slowly past the soldier, who, seeing the object approach, quickly stood upon his guard. But a well-

▲ Woodland Indians were masters of stealth and concealment, skills learned from years of hunting. Here a re-enactor illustrates how a deer skin could be used to break up the warrior's silhouette.

BATTLES IN THE EAST 1777–1858

The map below illustrates some of the major engagements fought between the Native Americans and the settlers from 1777 to 1858. Initially, the Indians in the east had the tactical advantage, but weight of settler numbers and attrition gradually took their toll. By the late 1850s, all of the Eastern territories were subdued by the settlers, the Native American tribes either destroyed, displaced further west or relocated onto reservations. 1858 saw the final subjugation of the Seminole, after a series of three wars.

known grunt eased his fears, and he suffered it to pass, it being too dark for any one to discover the cheat. The beast quietly sought the thicket to the left; it was nearly out of sight, when through a sudden break in the clouds, the moon shone bright upon it. The soldier then perceived the ornamental moccasin of a Savage, and quick as thought prepared to fire. But, fearing lest he might have been mistaken, and thus falsely alarm the camp – and also supposing, if it were so, other Savages would be near at hand, he refrained, and, having a perfect knowledge of Indian subtility, quickly took off his coat and cap, and, after hanging them on the stump where he had reclined, took hold of his rifle, and softly groped his way towards the thicket. He had barely reached it, when the whizzing of an arrow passed his head, and told him of the danger he had so narrowly escaped.'

– Turner (1836)

The techniques employed by the Indian here would not disgrace a modern special forces sniper, and only the American soldier's quick-thinking appears to have saved his life. Furthermore, the Indians were more prepared to use daylight and seasonal conditions to aid their operations. For example, when Narrangansett Indians aided the English in an attack on a local Pequot camp, they moved in at night, when the Pequot would be unprepared and mostly confined in their homes.

The Battle of Bloody Brook

A good example of how effective the Woodland Indians could be in ambush comes from King Philip's War (1675–76), one of the bloody seventeenth-century conflicts that blighted relations between the Native Americans and the New

Oriskany (1777)
Cherry Valley (1777)
Thames (1813)
Blackhawk War (1832)
Fallen Timbers (1794)
Wyoming Valley (1778)
● FORT DEFIANCE
FORT NECESSITY
Tippecanoe (1811)
King's Mountain (1780)
Cowpens (1781)
Creek War (1813–14)
Horseshoe Bend (1814)
ATLANTIC OCEAN
Fort Mims (1813)
First Seminole War (1817–19)
Dade's Massacre (1835)
Second Seminole War (1835–42)
Third Seminole War (1855–58)

◄ **King Philip, also known as Metacom, leader of the Wampanoag Indians, led his tribe during the bitter King Philip's War of 1675–76. The bold Indian attempt to drive out the settlers from Massachusetts initially succeeded, but the tide turned in 1675 and it is estimated that by the time defeat came, 15 per cent of the Wampanoag had been killed.**

settlers in Massachusetts. A particular grievance of the Wampanoag was the foundation of the town of Swansea, located just 6.4km (4 miles) away from Philip's home settlement, in the mid-1660s. On 20 June 1675, Wampanoag warriors attacked Swansea, and so began a round of tit-for-tat violence that would roll on for more than a year.

A notable action during the war was the battle of Bloody Brook, fought on 18 September 1675. It provides a textbook example of the effectiveness of Indian assault tactics. The burgeoning war had resulted in many colonists having to evacuate their towns, which were classed as at risk of falling to the Indians. Unfortunately, the very act of evacuation presented the Wampanoag with superb opportunities for ambush against the slow-moving columns of soldiers and civilians. One such column was led by Captain

England colonists. The conflict also provides a useful insight into how the wars between Indians and settlers often progressed. Its causes were familiar enough – settler expansionism, Christian proselytizing, then the collapse of local trade relations brought Chief Philip of the Wampanoag tribe into conflict with the British

Thomas Lathrop, who was escorting a load of cut wheat bound for the town of Hadley, where a British garrison was helping to provide protection for villages and evacuees. The route to their journey took them through an area of swampland 10km (6 miles) south of the town, bisected by a brook – perfect ambush

▲ **Lithograph of Arthur St Clair's Defeat (1791), in the opening stages of the battle with North American Indians near Fort Wayne, Ohio. The battle was a major Indian victory, and some 600 Americans dead.**

terrain in which the Indians concealed themselves ready for action. Swampland of any description was always threatening to the settlers, as it dramatically slowed movement while the Indians themselves moved around the landscape easily in their soft moccasins, which served to deaden the noise of footfalls. An early British settler in Massachusetts, Samuel Gorton, had actually described swampland as 'more pernicious to valiant souldiers then are bullwarkes, towers, castles, and walled cities.' It was a dangerous place through which to move, but there was complacency among the British ranks. The British column was a substantial one, and Lathrop had 80 soldiers under his command, all armed with muskets. Yet as the column slowed to cross the brook, a force of Wampanoag warriors suddenly burst from their hiding places around the swamp and opened a withering fire upon the British soldiers, using well-aimed musket fire and archery. During the attack, the Indians illustrated the classic principles of Native American firepower – spot a target, shoot it, then get back into cover while selecting another target. In this instance, such was the confidence of the fire that some 64 colonists were killed.

The noise of the exchange brought nearby British reinforcements, a unit of infantrymen led by Major Robert Treat and Captain Samuel Moseley, supported by a band of Mohegan Indians. Yet at this point the other element of Indian warfare came into play – the tactical retreat. Rather than engage the superior force, and with the element of surprise lost, they simply vanished back into the wilderness. The British soldiers moved back to Deerfield, where during the night they could hear the Indians taunting them from nearby woodland. In the end, Deerfield was simply abandoned and the town was burnt the ground.

The Battle of the Wabash

Perhaps the most illustrative example of Native Americans dominating regular forces came at the Battle of the Wabash (also known as St Clair's Defeat) on 4 November 1791. The context to the battle was the 1783 Treaty of Paris, which placed the territory east and south of the Great Lakes under US sovereignty. Naturally, the local Native Americans were not party to the treaty, and so began a campaign of regular violence against the Americans, with 1500 white settlers killed during the second half of the 1780s. Finally, the government of President Washington had had enough, and assembled a force of 1453 regular soldiers to go out and crush the Indian insurrection, the formation marching on 7 October 1790 commanded by Brigadier General Josiah Harmar. Battle was first joined near present-day Fort Wayne, Indiana, when some 400 American soldiers crossed swords with 1100 Indians, Harmar refusing to commit his full resources. The result was 223 American casualties, and the first defeat of the campaign. Indian casualties were similar, but they had taken the tactical initiative and put a severe dent in American martial confidence.

The next year, therefore, Washington ordered a renewed offensive, this time under the command of Arthur St Clair, a capable Seven Years' War veteran and governor of the Northwest territories. St Clair had a total of 2000 men, but they were of indifferent quality. Desertion cost his command 1800 men between September and November 1791. Many of the soldiers were part-time militia with scant experience of weapons handling and poor understanding of tactics and woodland survival. At dawn break on 4 November 1791, the motley force was encamped near what is today Fort Recovery, Ohio, near the Wabash River, unaware that a confederacy of some 1000 Indian warriors – Cherokee, Chippewas, Shawnees, Delawares, Mingos and others, led by the chiefs Little Turtle and Blue Jacket – was watching them and waiting to attack.

Devastating Attack

When the attack came, it was devastating. The Indian forces surged down to the perimeter of the American lines, using cover and concealment all the way. They set up a withering and accurate musket fire, thinning the ranks of the Americans as the regular soldiers and militia grabbed for their own stacked muskets. The American troops finally managed to establish some manner of traditional defensive line, and sent volleys of fire hissing through the undergrowth. They even managed to bring some cannon fire into play, although the canister shot flew too high, and simply went over the heads of the attacking Indians. Whatever firepower the Americans could generate had little effect – a musket ball could not get through the thick trees and earthen banks that the Indians were using for fire positions. Moreover, the attackers had deployed in a loose U-shaped formation around the American camp, and did not present the uniform ranks that were the best targets for volley fire.

Sensing their defeat, the American soldiers mounted a bayonet charge, but in response the Indians simply fell back and then circled around to cut off the charging soldiers from the camp. Eventually St Clair – one of the few officers left alive, although he had nearly been killed on several occasions – finally ordered a retreat, and those that could fled into the surrounding woodlands. The action had been a

SHAWNEE WARRIOR

This Shawnee Indian warrior is dressed in a style typical of the eighteenth and nineteenth centuries. A cotton shirt provides the base garment, with an overwrapped blanket for warmth. The hair style – shaven except for a tuft of hair left on the crown – often incorporated braided locks and feather decoration. He carries a self-bow and three metal-tipped arrows.

MOHAWK WARRIOR

This Mohawk warrior, bearing traditional facial tattoos, wears a metal gorget around his neck and has a dagger in a scabbard attached to his cross-straps. The pouch on the hip would have contained powder and balls for the flintlock musket, plus other supplies.

spectacular victory for the Indians – 600 Americans dead as opposed to 21 Indians – and a dose of reality for the US military.

The Second Seminole War

Throughout the seventeenth, eighteenth and nineteenth centuries, the Indians consistently played to their strengths against the Americans weaknesses. Although the were unable to 'win the war', they nevertheless secured enough victories in battle to trouble the settlers seriously. This was evident in the series of three Seminole Wars fought in Florida between 1816 and 1858, focused on the US government's attempts to control, subdue or expel the Seminole Indians from their traditional lands. The Second Seminole War of 1835–42 is particularly interesting from a tactical perspective, not least because of the abilities of one of the Seminole leaders, Osceola. Osceola's leadership skills comprehensively dismiss the idea that Indian warfare was rudimentary. Indeed, he seems to combine the Indian skills of guerrilla warfare with a more conventional understanding of how to inflict maximum damage on the enemy's ability to wage war.

For example, Osceola recognized that the various Seminole tribes would be much more effective if they coordinated their activities, so established a system of assistant commanders and of rapid inter-tribal communications, which allowed him to channel his forces quickly against emerging weak points. Furthermore, he understood that the logistically heavy Americans, with their need for substantial food, artillery and ammunition trains, were highly

OSCEOLA (C.1803–38)

Born into the Seminole in c.1803, Osceola gained early experience of combat fighting in the First Seminole War (1816–18), and rose to become a tribal leader by the early 1830s. During this time, Osceola resisted the US government's efforts to shift his people to Indian Territory (Oklahoma), and killed some prominent Seminole leaders who advocated the relocation. Osceola led his tribe in a guerilla war against the Americans for two years, inflicting serious casualties on the settlers through intelligent guerrilla warfare. In October 1837, however, he was duped into attending apparent peace discussions with the US commander General Thomas Jesup and was arrested upon his arrival. He was imprisoned near Charleston, and died there on 30 January 1838.

HORSESHOE BEND 1814

The battle of Horseshoe Bend in 1814 was a major Native American defeat in the Creek War (1813-14). Assisted by a large group of Cherokee Indians, future US President Andrew Jackson led a force of US troops against a Red Sticks Creek encampment in the Horseshoe Bend of the Tallapooa River. While the US soldiers formed the 'hammer' from the north, the allied Indians created the 'anvil' to the south, resulting in 750 Red Sticks killed out of a total force of 900 warriors.

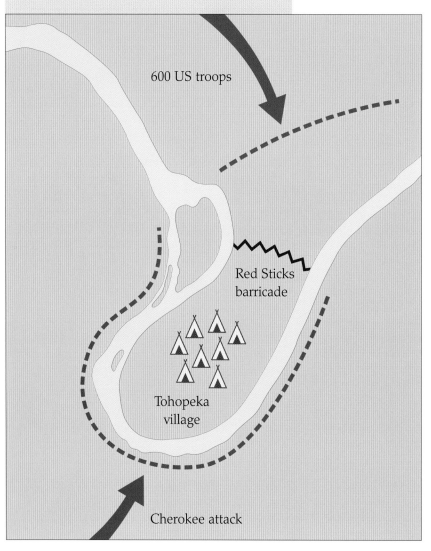

600 US troops

Red Sticks barricade

Tohopeka village

Cherokee attack

dependent on stable lines of communication. Hence he would not only ambush American columns, but he would also order bridges to be burnt, slowing down American response times to attacks elsewhere. On other occasions, he would launch raids on ill-protected civilian plantations, forcing the Americans to redeploy forces to tactically insignificant locations.

Eastern Indians, like all other Native Americans, placed a high value on personal bravery and the demonstration of the warrior spirit. Despite Osceola being the leader of the resistance, he obviously did not neglect these obligations. An official US report into the battle of Ouithlecoochee in 1836, in which Osceola personally led an ambush against an American column, pays genuine respect to the chief's martial bravery:

"Osceola was observed foremost of all his men in this battle, and was well known to General Clinch and many of his men. He wore a red belt, and three long feathers. Having taken his stand behind a tree, he would step boldly out, level his rifle, and bring down a man at every fire; nor was he dislodged until several volleys from whole platoons had been fired upon him. The tree behind which he stood was literally cut to pieces. It is almost a wonder that he had not now fulfilled the measure of his threat made on a former occasion, which was to kill General Clinch. He probably tried his best to do it, for the general received several shots through his clothes. General Thompson, Charles Omathla,

▲ An attack on Fort King by Native Americans under Osceola during the Seminole Wars, 1835. If the Indians couldn't take a main fortification, they would often set fire to outlying buildings.

and General Clinch were the three persons he had declared vengeance against.'

This account bears testimony to the Indian skill with firearms, Osceola managing to 'bring down a man with every fire'. In doing so it illustrates the disparity between American and Indian fire tactics. From the Indian side, each man is taking individual aimed shots, and the threat against General Clinch indicates that officers were specific targets for the Indian marksmen. In contrast, the US soldiers are firing coordinated platoon volleys at single targets, a major waste of ammunition, especially

▼ **Ambush - the shooting of General Braddock at Fort Duquesne, Pittsburgh, 1755. Note both the fast movement of the attackers between pieces of solid cover, and the individualistic approach to selecting targets, officers being primary victims.**

against someone behind a tree, which would have been perfectly resistant to contemporary musket ball ammunition.

Raiding

The example of the Seminole Wars shows that the Eastern Indians were capable of sustained organized resistance, not just localized raiding, although the latter did form an important constant in the martial life of a tribe. One of the best descriptions of the distinction between raiding and outright war is from William Kessel and Robert Wooster's *Encyclopedia of Native American Wars & Warfare*:

'For the most part, raids were designed to search out and procure enemy property. Raiding expeditions were generally directed by an experienced leader and were formed by as few as five to 15 or more men.

▲ **Indian warriors massacre a settler column, the close-quarters killing done with ball-and-spike war clubs. Such columns were extremely vulnerable to Indian attack, as they invariably used well-worn trails that were prone to ambushes.**

Traveling quietly they would locate an enemy and with as much stealth as possible take enemy possessions and occasionally enemy lives. Wars, on the other hand, involved much more organization and planning. An experienced war chief often led the expedition of many men. The primary purposes of wars were to avenge deaths and kill the enemy. Both raids and wars also provided opportunities for novices as well as experienced warriors to gain personal prestige.'

— *Kessel and Wooster* (2005)

Raiding had various purposes, but as Kessel and Wooster here imply, the raid was primarily a short-term tactical action rather than part of a prolonged strategic campaign (although the raid could contribute to such a campaign). During a small-scale action against another tribe, the clash between rival warriors might take on an almost ritualistic feel. The two sides might face each other openly, firing the occasional arrow, exchanging insults or even compliments, then draw together in a group for a brief clash of arms, resulting in a few injuries or perhaps even a death or two among the combatants.

Yet the raid could take on considerable proportions of up to (although rarely) 1000 men or more, especially when it was directed at an enemy fort or village, and could have more serious consequences for one side or the other. Such a major expedition could take on a festive feel, with multiple groups of warriors joining loosely together to journey to the target.

Attacking Fortifications

If facing a fortification, the attackers essentially had two options – direct or indirect assault, the latter often implying siege tactics. Some of the best explored examples of Indian versus Indian assaults relate to Iroquois attacks on Huron or French fortifications during the seventeenth century. For the direct assault, the Iroquois would literally run up to the outer defences of the fortification, moving as fast as possible to minimize exposure to enemy musketeers and bowmen firing from behind their barricades. While closing up to the fort, their own gunners and bowmen would lay down suppressing fire against the defenders, relying particularly on the shock value of their guns to

intimidate the enemy. Note that the attackers initially would have approached the fortification by stealth. This was no reenactment of European medieval city assaults, when the defenders would have been aware of the clanking, noisy attackers well in advance of their arrival. The Iroquois are also recorded as using armour to protect themselves from projectile weapons as they

closed up to the enemy defences. Thick, wooden hand-held shields were carried, dense enough to stop a musket ball, or several warriors carried a portable screen to protect them as they advanced.

Once the warriors arrived at the wall, they obviously had to gain access. There were two primary options. First, the attackers could set about the walls with their hatchets, cutting through the wooden defences to create a hole big enough to push warriors through. The second route into the fortification was by using scaling devices to climb over the tops of the walls. Scaling ladders were one option, these being light-framed ladders made from boughs lashed together with rawhide or similar materials. The protective screen mentioned above might also be leaned against the defences, the warriors using it as a step to gain access. Any other means of getting in would be used – there are records of upturned canoes being used to give a step up into enemy forts.

Indirect Approach

A frontal assault of a fortified village or outpost could be costly in terms of casualties, particularly if the fortification was equipped with cannon (primarily in the case of American outposts), which made short work of the wooden shields and armour of the attackers. The indirect approach, therefore, could be the wiser but more time-consuming option. In some instances, the fortification was simply encircled and laid siege to. This had its risks and costs – the besieging group would have to spend time away from their tribal subsistence duties, and there was always the threat of attack from reinforcements. Yet the indirect assault method provided several other options. The attackers could conduct frequent but persistent small-scale raids against the fortification, steadily nibbling away at the defences and defenders until the habitation became unviable. Any unprotected buildings, or food supplies

◀ **This stylized nineteenth-century view of a Seminole attack on an American blockhouse deprives the Native American warriors of the rapid movement they employed in the attack. Note, however, the irregular pattern of Indian musketry; they indeed avoided the volley fire often used by the settler armies.**

outside the habitation would be destroyed, or the attackers would target enemy foraging parties as they ventured out. Alternatively, the attackers might conduct an assault on a nearby but unprotected village, forcing the defenders of the fortified village to venture out to provide assistance, where they could be engaged in the open.

Fort Denonville

A classic example of the indirect assault approach is that of the Iroquois campaign against the French-occupied Fort Denonville in 1687–88. The Governor of New France, Jacques-Rene de Brisay, Marquis de Denonville, established the fort in 1687 as part of his campaign to oust the Iroquois from the Great Lakes, a campaign that did little more than incite the Indians to retaliate. Instead of attacking the fort, the Indians simply increased their hostile presence around the garrison, making it dangerous for those inside to venture out.

In effect, the garrison became besieged, a state of affairs made worse by the onset of winter and their distance from reinforcements and resupply from Montreal. The Iroquois imposed disease and starvation conditions on the French soldiers, keeping them trapped and without reinforcements until Denonville was forced to abandon the fort altogether. Such was the Iroquois threat that it would be more than three decades before the French were able to maintain a presence on the Niagara. Attacks on fortifications illustrate that the Indian 'way of war' did in fact include major operations focused on strategic gain, and not just loose strategies of raiding.

Defeat From Victory

Pursuing Indians, often after they had retreated during an attack, also soaked up American energy and

> 'IT WAS THOUGHT, IF THEIR CORN WERE CUT DOWN, THEY WOULD STARVE AND DIE WITH HUNGER; AND ALL THAT COULD BE FOUND WAS DESTROYED, AND THEY DRIVEN FROM THAT LITTLE THEY HAD IN STORE, INTO THE WOODS, IN THE MIDST OF WINTER; AND YET HOW TO ADMIRATION DID THE LORD PRESERVE THEM FOR HIS HOLY ENDS, AND THE DESTRUCTION OF MANY STILL AMONG THE ENGLISH!'
>
> – ROWLANDSON (1682)

supplies, particularly on account of the endurance of which the Indians were capable. Compared to the European settlers, the Indians were incredibly light on their feet in terms of logistics. A European column, not being trained to live off the land, would rely heavily on cumbersome supply trains, winding arduously throughout the convoluted tracks that twisted through the Eastern woodlands.

The Indians, by contrast, could live off the land in which they had hunted from their earliest years. Furthermore, their nimbleness of foot and knowledge of the local terrain meant that they were not constrained to travel along familiar routes. Their dietary requirements would almost equate to starvation rations for most Europeans. The captive Mary Rowlandson, held prisoner by the Indians and whisked along with her family at a brisk pace, was startled to see the efficiency with which they could feed themselves in the most barren of landscapes. She admits to earlier prejudices.

Rowlandson acknowledges that contemporary wisdom taught that destroying an Indian tribe's central food resources would result in the death of a people. In a sense she is right – as we shall see, sustained community existence was threatened by the European encroachment into Indian food sources. Yet in terms of the warrior himself, on operations, this was far from the case. Rowlandson goes on to explain how the Indians sourced nutrition on their arduous journey:

'Their chief and commonest food was groundnuts, they eat also nuts and acorns, artichokes, lilly roots, ground beans, and several other weeds and roots that I know not. They would pick up old bones, and cut them in pieces at the joints, and if they were full of worms and maggots, they would scald them over the fire, to make the vermine come out, and then boil

FORTIFICATION ASSAULT
Iroquois warriors are here seen executing an attack on an enemy tribe's fortified village. On the approach to the fortification walls, the warriors protect themselves from arrows and (to a degree) musket balls by using wooden shields, which could be both multi-person or individual varieties. Canoes used for deployment could also provide some cover and a stepping platform for ascending the walls. Other warriors hack open the walls with tomahawks, creating access or firing holes.

them, and drink up the liquor, and then beat the great ends of them in a mortar, and so eat them. They would eat horses guts, and ears, and all sorts of wild birds which they could catch: Also bear, venison, beavers, tortoise, frogs, squirrels, dogs, skunks, rattle-snakes: Yea the very bark of trees; besides all sorts of creatures, and provision which they plundered from the English; I can but stand in admiration to see the wonderful power of God, in providing for such a vast number of our enemies in the wilderness, where there was nothing to be seen, but from hand to mouth. Many times in the morning, the generality of them would eat up all

they had, and yet have some farther supply against they wanted. But now our perverse and evil carriages in the sight of the Lord, have so offended him, that instead of turning his hand against them, the Lord feeds and nourishes them up to be a scourge to the whole land.'
– *Rowlandson* (1682)

Note the following comment in Paul Wellman's 1934 publication *The Indian Wars of the West*:

'The Indian [was thought] as less than human and worthy only of extermination. We did shoot down defenseless men, and women and children at places like Camp Grant, Sand Creek, and Wounded Knee. We did feed strychnine to red warriors. We did set whole villages of people out naked to freeze in the iron cold of Montana winters. And we did confine thousands in what amounted to concentration camps.'

—Wellman (1934)

It is hard to imagine, even with the frequent brutality of Indian behaviour towards their enemies, this perspective existing in a tribal context. Indians would go on to destroy and displace, but the enemy was frequently accorded a notional respect, and objectives of military action tended to be land and horses, not the destruction of an entire people. The Eastern or other Native American tribes also had military weaknesses when compared to the settler Americans. First, the Indians never manufactured firearms or gunpowder themselves. This left them at the mercy of supplies from the Europeans, which could be controlled according to government agendas. The rapacious Europeans would also take over prime hunting or agricultural land, forcing the tribe to move on or disperse. Finally, the Native Americans were never a united force against the Europeans, as the Civil War demonstrated. Various alliances came and went, leaving them prey to the Europeans who could eventually marshal huge military manpower and federal unity.

▲ **The death of Shawnee leader Tecumseh at the battle of the Thames in 1813. Note the way that the Indian on the left attacks the horse with his tomahawk; the Indians quickly realized that mounts could be more vulnerable than riders.**

This is a natural point to return to the fact that although the Indians fought a good fight, it was not enough to retain their lands or, in many cases, survive. There are several important reasons why this is so. Partly, as has been suggested already, the American Indians were excellent at fighting local wars, or settling temporary tribal clashes, but their mindset was not the same as that of the Europeans, which by the late nineteenth century had a 'total war' inflexion.

CIVIL WAR SERVICE

The ability of the Native Americans to live off the land as Rowlandson describes was integral to their success in war. It was their very skills in tracking and survival that led to the recruitment of large numbers of Native Americans as scouts in the US military forces. During the Civil War of 1861–65, nearly 29,000 Native Americans served on the side of either the Confederacy or the Union. In this role, the Indians were hybrid soldiers, often donning official issue military dress but with recognizable Indian elements, such as wielding tomahawks and scalping knives alongside their rifles.

Most of the Eastern Indian tribes were participants in the conflict in one way or another, hardly surprising since the primary battlefields were in the Eastern territories of the United States. This in itself weakened the Indian grip over the territories, either through compromising themselves in disadvantageous treaties with the losing Confederate side, or through factionalism brought about by different positions on the conflict. The Cherokee, for example, were already divided into several factions by the time of the Civil War, with each having a different position on relations with the settlers. Having been promised national independence by the Confederacy, most of the Cherokee allied themselves with the South. While the war raged, the Cherokee proved to be excellent allies of the Confederacy, especially in conducting guerilla-style warfare. On 19 September 1864, for example, Cherokee troops of the Indian Cavalry Brigade (under the leadership of charismatic leader Stand Watie) inflicted 200 casualties on the Union at the Second Battle of Cabin Creek, also capturing 129 supply wagons,

▲ A studio portrait of Stand Watie (1806–71). A three-quarter Cherokee, he lead the tribe, who allied themselves with the Confederacy. At the end of the war he held the rank of brigadier-general in the Confederate Army.

740 mules and taking 120 prisoners. A composite unit of Eastern tribes also formed Company K of the 1st Michigan Sharpshooters, earning distinction in famous battles such as Wilderness, Spotsylvania and Crater. Yet service in the Civil War proved to be a poisoned chalice for many Native American forces. For the Cherokee, for example, the war depleted their already dwindling population by 6000 men, and at the end of the war their support for the Confederacy earned them the distaste of the Federal Government, and later acts and treaties saw their land ownership effectively annulled.

CHAPTER 2

Northern Tribes

The tribes of the northern United States and Canada occupied territories ranging from lush plains through to Arctic tundra. Those Indians in the northern extremes often managed to preserve their way of life longer than the Indians of the east or south, but eventually the depredations of the settlers caught up with them.

It is evident from surviving eighteenth- and nineteenth-century American literature that the Native Americans living in Canada were often viewed with the same disdain and horror as Indian tribes living elsewhere in North America. The following passage of text comes from an encyclopedia entitled *The Youth's Companion*, compiled and written by Ezra Sampson in 1813, which leaves the reader under no illusions about his impression of the Indians north of the Canadian border:

'Canada Indians, tribes as fierce and warlike as any of the aborigines of North America. During a great part of the time that Canada was a province of the French government, which was from its first settlement till its conquest by the British in

◀ **Fort McKenzie, 28 August 1833. A group of Assiniboine and Cree indians attack a Blackfoot encampment. The weapons are a mix of the traditional and the modern, with spears and short bows used alongside flintlock muskets.**

1759, the frontiers of the colonies of New-York, Massachusetts and New-Hampshire, were frequently infested by those savages. In the depth of winter, 1689, a party of those Indians, together with a number of Frenchmen, surprized the town of Schenectady, in the night, while the inhabitants were unalarmed and in a profound sleep; and butchered them, with circumstances of most horrible barbarity. The whole village was instantly in a blaze; women with child were ripped open, and their infants cast into the flames. Sixty persons perished in the massacre, and twenty-seven were carried into captivity, the rest fled naked through the snow to Albany.'

– *Ezra Sampson* (1813)

Making no concessions to his young readership, Sampson goes on in a similar vein for the entire entry, making garish descriptions of children having 'their brains beat out against the trees' and women being disembowelled. Yet as with so many colonial sketches of the Native Americans, Sampson is keen to emphasize the horrors at the expense of the more sophisticated aspects of Canadian Indian culture, and their techniques of waging war.

The geographical reach of this chapter is extensive. Chapter 1 has already touched upon the Iroquois and Algonquian tribes of eastern North America, which extended their territories out of the Great Lakes, Quebec and the Maritimes. In this chapter we will range to the west and north, taking in the Indian

▲ An Assiniboine village, consisting of loosely gathered tipis. Scalps hang from wooden frames outside, signifying earlier victories and declaring the bravery and martial talents of the tipi occupants. Note also the carrying frame attached to the dog in the foreground, which was used to carry weapons as well as supplies on long-distance raids.

tribes from what is today the Canadian–US border up to the Alaskan homelands of the Inuit. There is something of an overlap with the next chapter, which focuses on the Plains Indians, a 'culture area' that did itself extend into eastern and central Canada. Tribes such as the Cree and Blackfoot, for example, are generally classed as Plains Indians, but they will also

▲ **A Chippewa chief, seen wearing decorative sashes over his tasselled buckskin shirt and a string of** *wampum* **beads. The Chippewa were steadily displaced from their lands during the eighteenth and nineteenth centuries.**

be studied in this chapter, not only for their influence on northern North America, but also because their territories embraced a wide spectrum of terrain, including Canadian mountains and forests. The physical landscape of this region, as we shall see, had a key impact on the type of warfare practised by the indigenous inhabitants.

In the massive Canadian forests, for example, we see styles of warfare similar to those exhibited by the Woodland tribes of the east. Moving further north into the subarctic, however, the severe restrictions of climate and terrain shaped a much more localized and temporary style of conflict, on account of the environment being just as dangerous as any human enemy.

TRIBES OF THE NORTH

The term 'Northern Tribes' covers a large range of tribal territories and peoples. Note that when describing the Native Americans of Canada, excluding the Inuit and the Métis – descendants of marriages between Native Americans and European settlers – it is more correct to refer to the 'First Nations', a term that covers all aboriginal peoples in Canada stretching back to the Stone Age. As we are including Alaska in this chapter, however, we will use 'Northern' to refer to all Indian people around and north of the Canadian border. They included the Algonquin,

Nipissing, Montagnais and Naskapi north of the Great Lakes and up to the Hudson Bay region; the Cree, Chippewa and Algonquin dominating Canada's central regions; the Blackfoot, Ojibway and Assiniboine straddling the Canadian–US border; and the Inuit and Yellowknife occupying the subarctic northern extremes.

In the period covered by this book (1500–1890), the most profound challenge to most of these Northern tribes was the same as that of the US tribes – contact with the colonizing Europeans. During the sixteenth century, both the French and the British

CHIPPEWA INDIAN
A Chippewa Indian chief, here seen armed with a simple war club, carved from a single piece of wood, and a long spear. The long and well-crafted metal spearhead indicates a post-contact time. Before contact with the settlers and the introduction of metals, the Native Americans tended to tip their spears either through a basic process of fire-hardening, or through the manufacture of chipped flint spearheads.

made regular visits to Canada's eastern shorelines, their appetites whetted by excellent fishing and the ability to trade European goods with the Native Americans in return for high-quality furs (particularly beaver).

Yet while the British focused most of their colonial muscle on what is today the eastern seaboard of the United States, it was the French who became the dominant foreign settlers in Canada. By the early decades of the seventeenth century, 'New France' was beginning to take shape, spurred by Samuel de Champlain's foundation of the city of Québec in 1608. Champlain knew that the fragility of the French colonies in a hostile wilderness necessitated making alliances with the local Indians. On this basis, he allied himself with the Algonquin, Huron and Montagnais against the Iroquois, and these tribes would also later assist the French in fighting British expansion.

CANADA AND ALASKA: TRIBAL AREAS

The map here shows the major tribal territories of Canada and Alaska, at least in terms of the traditional tribal areas before the displacements caused by settler expansion. The fortunes of the tribes varied according to their geographical location and also their relations with the settlers. No tribal area was entirely free from settler interference. The tribes of subarctic Canada, for example, came into contact with traders for the Hudson's Bay Company during the 1670s, and suffered a consequent loss of major fur resources to the Europeans. Alaskan Indians encountered not only settlers pushing up from the south, but also, for a time, Russian traders coming into North America across the Bering Strait.

HURON
A statue of a Huron-Algonquin Indian from explorer Samuel de Champlain's group overlooks the Ottawa River. He carries a quiver of arrows on his back. The French had a variable relationship with the Native Americans they encountered.

The Beaver Wars

The influx of European colonists, therefore, brought broader hostility between Indian tribes, not just between tribes and settlers. A particularly bitter outpouring of this dissension was the so-called Beaver Wars (1635–84). Trade in beaver furs was a major source of income for the Iroquois and neighbouring Huron. Yet such was the demand for furs from Europe that by the 1630s the supply of these animals in the eastern parts of North America was starting to dry up. Yet around the Great Lakes, controlled by the French and the allied Huron, the beaver had managed to maintain its population levels.

The result was war between the Iroquois and the Huron, as the former attempted to move in on the latter's beaver grounds, burning Huron villages and killing both Huron and French citizens. A major Iroquois invasion of Huron territory, 1000 warriors strong, in March 1649 resulted in the destruction of the towns of St Ignace and St Louis, near modern Toronto, and the mass exodus of Huron Indians from their homelands. Sensing their own power, the Iroquois then attacked other tribes in the Great Lakes region, their war parties sometimes rising to nearly 2000 warriors, before spreading down the Ohio Valley, eventually commanding territories from the Ottawa River to Kentucky. As with so many Native American wars, however, success in battle did not bring

victory in the overall war. During the 1680s, various tribes, with French assistance, began to claw back their territories around the western Great Lakes and east of the Mississippi. In the Canadian territories, the Chippewa pushed back the Iroquois from around Lake Ontario, and the Iroquois were forced to retreat and finally admit defeat.

Even as the Iroquois were attempting to enforce their monopoly over the fur trade, New France was expanding and consolidating itself, albeit while increasing the friction between French and British imperial interests. At its height in the early eighteenth century, New France stretched from Newfoundland to the Rocky Mountains and from Hudson Bay to the Gulf of Mexico.

Its northern possessions were divided into four main regions; Canada, Acadia, Hudson Bay and Newfoundland (Plaisance). The colonial map changed with the French and Indian War of 1754–63, part of

▲ 'They See A Lightening Flash And Hear A Roar.' Samuel de Champlain (1567–1635) defeats a group of Iroquois with the help of the Algonquins, 1609. The Indians would soon become accustomed to firepower.

the globally engulfing Seven Years' War (1756–63) between the British and French empires.

The British won out eventually, and from 1764 to 1867, Canada remained under British imperial control (borders between Canada and the United States were first formally established in 1783 following the American Revolution), although their rights of possession were tested by conflicts such as the War of 1812 and a series of rebellions in Canada.

The Cree

It is little wonder, given the state of frequent conflict in North America, that the Northern Indian tribes found themselves struggling for survival. One of the largest tribes in terms of numbers and territorial

▲ Two Native Americans and three settlers paddle a canoe on Lake George, New York, during the French and Indian War. Native American guides and scouts were essential to the settlers in an unfamiliar landscape.

◀ An Inuit Indian family cross a river in a traditional Native American canoe. Birchbark canoes could reach up to 7.3m (24ft) in length.

▼ A Native American canoe under construction. The skeleton frame of the canoe was usually made from a wood such as cedar, which was then covered with birchbark panels.

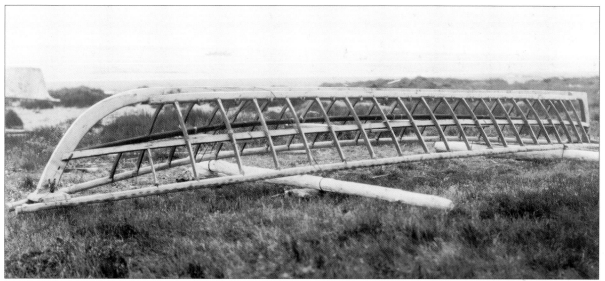

extent was the Cree, who at their greatest reach had homelands stretching from the Northwest territories down to the plains of Montana. The Cree came into contact with Europeans during the early 1600s, and saw the opportunity to make profitable trade connections with both the French and the British. The way of war amongst the Northern Cree prior to contact with the settlers was similar to that of the Eastern Indians. Conflicts consisted of short-lived ambushes and raiding parties designed to acquire patches of territory, settle scores or demonstrate warrior prowess.

The nomadic lifestyle of the Cree, moving camp according to season and hunting ground, meant that more sustained warfare was neither feasible nor relevant. Cree lived in tipis made of birch bark, pine branches and caribou hides, and they could move

camp quickly and easily. Among the Cree, therefore, we generally do not see the drive to create fortifications that we saw in the case of the Eastern tribes, although there are other examples of tribal palisade fortifications around the northern edges of the Great Lakes.

Cree males spent much of their time hunting game such as ducks, geese, moose, caribou, deer, beaver and hare, and the act of hunting was accompanied by much ritual and magic related to forest and animal spirits. This magic side to hunting later withered somewhat when the Cree moved further south and discovered seemingly endless supplies of buffalo on the Great Plains, making the spirits far less important in the acquisition of food and hides.

They could move with ease through the wilderness regardless of the season, using snowshoes in the

SIMPLE TRANSPORT
Canoes such as this one were perfect systems of transportation along the lakes and rivers of North America, especially as they were typically light enough for two or three men to carry once a group made landfall. Raiding parties might also take canoes into battle, tipping them over and using them as a basic form of barricade against arrows and spears.

winter and navigating the Canadian rivers in birch bark canoes. Their intimate knowledge of the flora, fauna and landscape meant that the Cree Indians were natural choices for guides and trappers for the British and French settlers. In particular, their interaction with settlers around the Hudson Bay area, a hub of transatlantic trade, meant that in return, the Cree received firearms, a new technology that changed their way of fighting forever.

BLACKFOOT RAIDERS

Before reflecting on the transition effected by firearms, we should widen our study to include another important Northern tribe, the Blackfoot. Blackfoot land was traditionally further west and south than that of the Cree, with a north–south range of the Saskatchewan River in Alberta, down to the plains of Montana, and reaching as far west as the Rocky Mountains.

Around 1800, the Blackfoot were estimated to number a minimum of 20,000 people (according to a report to the US Secretary of War), and they were much feared by both American settlers and associated tribes. American trappers encroaching into Blackfoot territory during the early 1800s did so at risk of their lives, and Blackfoot war parties were known for their extreme prejudice in going after their goals. Some war parties were known to travel hundreds of kilometres for an engagement. Yet the historian John C. Ewers has emphasized that like many Indian tribes, even the Blackfoot waged war with only limited aims:

'Nevertheless, Blackfoot warfare was aimed at neither the systematic extermination of enemy tribes nor the acquisition of their territory. It was not organized and directed by a central military authority, nor was it prosecuted by large, disciplined armies. Rather, Blackfoot warfare was carried on primarily by small parties of volunteers who banded together to capture horses from enemy tribes. Each raiding party was hastily organized before departure and disbanded immediately after its return home. It might never see action again as a military unit. Its members were motivated much less by tribal patriotism than by hope of personal gain – the economic security and social prestige that possession of a goodly number of horses would bring them. The killing of enemy tribesmen and the taking of scalps were not major objectives of these raids.'

– John C. Ewers (1958)

Preparation

Blackfoot warfare, therefore, was predatory but not overly destructive in its goals. To back up his point, Ewers described in detail the process of a horse-raiding party, a useful study for the general theme of horse raiding that occurs throughout this book. Raiding tended to be more common in the spring and summer months, as better weather made travelling

TIPI CONSTRUCTION

Ten to 20 poles made up the frame of a typical tipi, the poles being lashed at the top and positioned precisely on the ground at the bottom to map out the floor area. Bison or deer skins, or panels of canvas, formed the outer covering and were held in place by ropes and pegs attached to the wooden frame. An outlet for smoke was left at the top.

INSIDE A TIPI

Life inside a tipi was warm and communal. These habitations were vulnerable to attack, however, especially to arrows or firearms fired through smoke or entrance flaps.

easier, although Ewers points out that winter raids might be conducted because of the reduced vigilance of 'enemy' tribes and the sound-masking effects of deep snowfall. The party would be organized and led by an experienced warrior, who gathered volunteers for the raid. Participation was not compulsory, but there was doubtless some social pressure on a young man to join in unless he had good reason not to.

Typically the Blackfoot party would amount to around a dozen men. The raiders would not set out immediately, but would first have to ask and receive permission for the raid from the tribal chief, then participate in the ritualistic aspects of preparation. They would chant war songs to the rhythm of a skin drum, and gather supplies and clothing for the journey, often supplied by eager relatives. While the Eastern tribes, as we have seen, wore some heavy types of rigid body armour, the Blackfoot and most Northern and Plains tribes wore varieties of 'soft armour' – thick padded leather or multi-layer buckskin coats. These would later prove of little use against musket balls or bullets but, during their time, provided some measure of protection against arrows and spears.

Yet for many horse raids, especially those during the hot summer months, the raiders were likely to ride 'light' without any form of armour, wearing just their traditional buckskin clothing and moccasin footwear. Spare clothes were carried in a separate bag.

MOUNTED BLACKFOOT WARRIOR
A Blackfoot warrior shows his skills with a horse while carrying a musket. Although the Native Americans readily adopted both firearms and horses, the two were an awkward mix, especially if the warrior attempted to reload the flintlock gun on horseback. For this reason, Native Americans often stuck with their traditional bows when fighting from horses, until the percussion age.

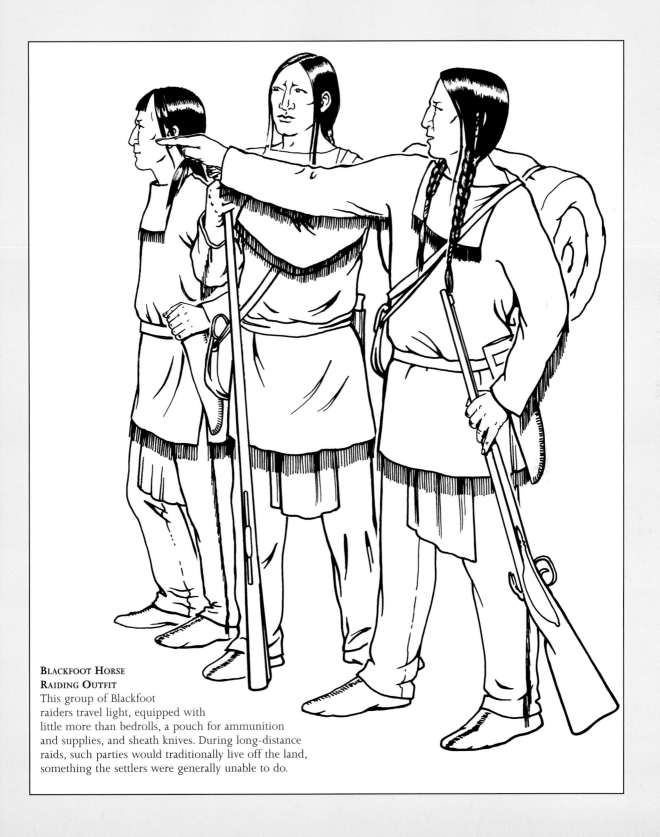

**BLACKFOOT HORSE
RAIDING OUTFIT**
This group of Blackfoot
raiders travel light, equipped with
little more than bedrolls, a pouch for ammunition
and supplies, and sheath knives. During long-distance
raids, such parties would traditionally live off the land,
something the settlers were generally unable to do.

In terms of weaponry, the Blackfoot raiding party would also avoid weighing themselves down with an unwarranted armoury. The raid, after all, was for acquiring horses rather than engaging in a long battle of attrition. Most warriors would carry a large knife in a sheath at his waist – the metal blades being one of the benefits of trade with the Europeans. This blade was as much a utility tool as a weapon, being used for making camp or cutting rawhide bindings, for example. In addition, the warrior also carried either a bow or a musket. Each weapon had its merits and drawbacks. The bow was lighter and had a higher rate of fire than the musket, but did not carry the shock

value, penetration or, with rifled weapons, the range and accuracy of the firearm. Bows also had the added advantage of silence – the noise of a gunshot could carry a long way on the plains and in the forests, and might alert the target tribe to the approaching war party. Some accounts speak of raiding parties leaving any firearms behind with the rest of the tribe, owing to both their value and their increasing usefulness for hunting.

War Lodges

Ewers notes that: 'On approaching enemy territory, the raiders stopped to kill enough game to provide food for the remainder of the journey. Usually they built a war lodge in a heavily timbered bottom or on a thickly wooded height, or repaired an old one built by some earlier party.' War lodges were not necessarily defensive fortifications *per se*, although they could be turned to that purpose if necessary, but were rather camouflaged and discreet refuges where the raiding party could recuperate and prepare. Nor were they only built by the Blackfoot – war lodges appear to be common among the Plains Indians, and were used by tribes such as the Cree, Sioux, Crow, Cheyenne and Arapaho (see the next chapter for more about the specifics of war on the Plains). The war lodge was a rather rough-and-ready construction. Constructed in a

◀ In this 1898 photograph, Assiniboine Chief Wets It is shown wearing the traditional feathered and horned headdress, plus a decorated shield. Shield construction varied, but often consisted of a thick disk of wood and/or animal hide.

INDIAN WAR PARTY
The Native American warriors of the far north were adept at coping with snowy conditions. The party here, moving out on a raiding operation, are all wearing snowshoes. Cree Indian snowshoes could measure up to nearly 1.8m (6ft) long, while those of tribes further north were typically shorter, and triangular or circular in shape. Spears were particularly common weapons of the Northern tribes, as they were used in the hunting of both aquatic and large land animals.

tipi shape, it was usually formed from three or four thick logs or boughs arranged in an upright, mutually supporting structure, with the 'walls' made from intertwined branches covered with overlapping sheets of cottonwood bark to provide waterproofing. Alternatively, the warriors might use similar principles to construct a rectangular version. Regardless of the final shape, the war lodge was generally made to blend into the wilderness and its status as a habitation was not apparent at a casual glance. The great American explorers Lewis and Clark, in their work *Travels to the Source of the Missouri River* (1815), recount the appearance of a typical war lodge (not Blackfoot):

'In one of the low bottoms of the river was an Indian fort, which seems to have been built during the last summer. It was built in the form of a circle, about fifty feet [15m] in diameter, five feet high [1.5m], and formed of logs, lapping over each other, and covered on the outside with bark set up on end. The entrance also was guarded by a work on each side of it facing the river. These entrenchments, the squaw informs us, are frequently made by the Minnetarees and other Indians at war with the Shoshonees, when pursued by their enemies on horseback.'

– *Lewis and Clark* (1815)

War lodges were essential for raiding parties. It must be remembered that raids were conducted against targets sometimes hundreds of kilometres from the warriors' home village, and the warriors might be living off the land for several weeks.

The Raid

When approaching the enemy's camp or village, the raiding party detached scouts to go out on reconnaissance, noting details such as enemy strength, weaponry, direction of travel, how many horses were available, and so on. The scouts then reported back to the leader, and a plan of attack was formed. As an attack was usually scheduled for dawn, the attackers would spend a fitful night going through pre-fight rituals, such as singing war songs, applying war paint, praying to the sun and moon for success in combat and putting on war medicine bundles. These bundles were typically pouches containing charms deemed to protect the warrior in battle and life. The objects within the bundles varied from pieces of fur and animal skin through to scalps and pipes. Bunches of feathers tied together might also constitute a medicine bundle (this style of bundle was common among the Blackfoot).

WAR PAINT

Native Americans applied war paint to the face and body for both spiritual and practical reasons. Spiritually, each tribe had its own symbolism that represented concepts of death (commonly evoked through black paint), bravery, success (often red paint), revenge, and so on. Applying these colours would inspire confidence, courage and resignation to the will of the spirits. The paint also carried talismanic qualities, supposedly helping to ward off enemy blows and missiles. The practical purpose of war paint was that in the heat of battle it helped the tribes to identify their own – something otherwise not easy in tribes with similar styles of dress.

▲ Ne-Sou-A Quoit, a Fox chief. His face is entirely covered in war paint, the dominant colour, red, likely indicating his success as a warrior on the field of battle, or making the intimidating suggestion of future spilt blood. The red colouring was produced by using ochre, a reddish clay, and was painted on using either tree-branch brushes or bone.

◄ The Blackfoot chief Mehkskeme-Sukahs, with blood patterns painted onto his face. Red was actually the most popular colour of war paint, owing to the wide availability of ochre. Black lines were also favoured, created by using a charcoal stick.

BLACKFOOT INDIANS WITH SHIELDS
Two Blackfoot warriors equipped with wooden medicine shields. Interestingly, the European settlers attempted to sell metal shields to the Blackfoot, but the Blackfoot largely rejected these. They felt that the metal shields were both an extravagance and were spiritually deficient.

BLACKFOOT MEDICINE SHIELD
A medicine shield was not only a tool of physical protection, it also contained spiritual protection for the warrior who carried it. The motifs and decorations on the shield held religious significance for the tribe, and each shield was usually blessed by the village shaman before it was allowed to go into battle.

Preparations complete, the warriors would then move in at dawn. The supreme achievement was to stalk silently into the enemy camp, cut the ties of the horses, and lead them equally silently out of the camp. Ewers notes that 'forty to sixty horses was considered a very good haul' for their troubles. If the enemy was not awakened during these efforts, the raiders would focus on covering as much ground as quickly as possible to put distance between them and the village – doubtless enemy warriors would set off in pursuit once the theft was discovered, and tracking several dozen fleeing horses was little problem for Native American scouts. If the raiding party was caught in the act, or during the subsequent pursuit, then it would have to fight.

When it came to combat, the raiders had surprise on their side, but usually little else, especially when raiding a well-populated village. Raiding parties were undoubtedly precarious affairs, not only threatening death in battle but also the prospect of death from disease or exposure during the long journey. In 1859, the American artist Paul Kane published an account of his travels among the Indian peoples of Canada, and described a Cree and a Blackfoot expedition that ended disastrously for the raiders.

A year before my arrival amongst them, a war party of 700 left for the Blackfeet country, which nation the Crees regard as their natural enemies, and are never at peace with them. After travelling for some fifteen or twenty days, a sickness broke out among them, affecting numbers and carrying off a few. This was considered by some of their great men a judgment upon them from the Great Spirit for some previous misconduct, and they, therefore, returned home without having accomplished anything. On another occasion a similar party fell in with a great warrior among the Blackfeet, named 'Big Horn', and six of his tribe, who were out on the legitimate calling of horse stealing – for the greater the horse thief the greater the warrior. This small band, seeing their inferiority to their enemies, attempted flight; but finding escape impossible, they instantly dug holes sufficiently deep to intrench themselves, from which they kept up a constant fire with guns and arrows, and for nearly twelve hours held at bay this large war party, bringing down every man who ventured within shot, until their

ammunition and arrows were entirely exhausted, when they of course fell an easy prey to their enemies, thirty of whom had fallen before their fire. This so enraged the Crees that they cut them in pieces, and mangled the dead bodies in a most brutal manner, and carried their scalps back as trophies.'

– *Kane (1859)*

Kane's account is an important corrective to some complacent notions about Native American warriors. Although they were often supremely in tune with the landscape, the experience of surviving in the wilderness was still depressingly hard, especially factoring in disease. In one winter alone (1839–40), for example, the Blackfoot lost some 8000 people to smallpox, and most other Indian tribes suffered from similar biological culls. Note also how in the case of the defending Blackfoot, they actually go to ground in what sound like shallow slit trenches. The response to their situation is very modern, and shows that they had no desire to sacrifice themselves needlessly. The Blackfoot capability with firearms is also apparent, and leads us to closer examination of how Indian warfare in general changed with the gun rather than the bow. As we shall see, the Northern Indians bought wholeheartedly into the use of firearms, but blended them with very traditional skills and tactics.

FROM BOWS TO FIREARMS

In the late eighteenth century, a chief of the Piegan tribe, Saukamappee, described a battle between the Piegan and Shoshone that took place in 1725 near Saskatoon, Saskatchewan. The account is remarkable for providing an insight into pre-contact Native American warfare, particularly the ritualistic aspects of

◀ **A nineteenth-century portrait of a northern Native American and his son. Note the thick mittens, which were often designed to allow operation of a firearm.**

NORTHERN SHIELDS

The following is a description from a French missionary, writing in 1633, describing a Canadian Indian's shield and its use:

'He bore with him a very large buckler, very long and very wide; it covered all my body easily, and went from my feet up to my chest. They raise it and cover themselves entirely with it. It was made of a single piece of very light cedar; I do not know how they can smooth so large and wide a board with their knives; it was a little bent or curved in order the better to cover the body, and in order that the strokes of arrows or of blows coming to split it should not carry away the piece, he had sewed it above and below with cord of skin; they do not carry the shields on the arm; they pass the cord which sustains them over the right shoulder, protecting the left side; and when they have aimed their blow they have only to draw back the right side to cover themselves.'

— Beauchamp (1905)

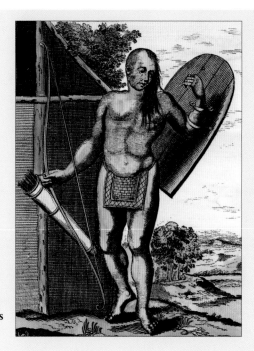

▶ **This seventeenth-century woodcut shows a Native American from the Great Lakes area holding a shield and bow, with arrows in a quiver.**

the clash, and also for describing the types of weapons and their use:

'A war chief was elected by the chiefs, and we got ready to march. Our spies had been sent out and had seen a large camp of the Snake [Shoshone] Indians on the Plains of the Eagle Hill, and we had to cross the river in canoes, and on rafts, which we carefully secured for our retreat. When we had crossed and numbered our men, we were about 350 warriors ... they had their scouts out, and came out to meet us. Both parties made a great show of their numbers, and I thought that they were more numerous than ourselves. After some singing and dancing, they sat down on the ground, and placed their large shields before them, which covered them. We did the same, but our shields were not so many, and some of our shields had to shelter two men. Theirs were all placed touching one another; their bows were not so long as ours, but of better wood, and the back covered with the sinews of the bisons which made them very elastic, and their arrows went a long way and whizzed about us as balls do from guns. They were all headed with a sharp, smooth, black stone which broke when

it struck anything. Our iron-headed arrows did not go through their shields, but stuck in them. On both sides, several were wounded, but none lay on the ground; and night put an end to the battle, without a scalp being taken on either side, and in those days such was the result, unless one party was more numerous than the other.'

In many ways the encounter seems purposely designed to avoid major casualties. The warriors present themselves openly, and then seemingly at some prearranged signal squat down behind shields to exchange arrows. Bows are the primary weapons. The Shoshone Indians shoot flint-headed arrows from sinew-backed bows, while the Piegan seem to be using self-bows. Sinew-backed bows improved the power of the bow by gluing a strip of elastic sinew to the inside of the bow – the sinew increased the whip effect when the bow was released, thereby imparting more power to the arrow. Typically, Northern bows were manufactured from ash or hickory, although some extant Northern bows have been found made from yew or osage orange – both excellent woods that grow well outside of the Northern territories, suggesting

▲ **Blackfoot warriors clash with Sioux Indians on the North American plains. Note the use of spears, shields, tomahawks and handguns, plus the martial decoration on the warriors' horses.**

that the Northern Indians would import high-quality bow woods when possible.

Once firearms spread throughout the Northern territories from the seventeenth century, however, this formalized picture of warfare changed significantly. For a start, the battle of opposing shield lines described above became suicidal for both sides, as the balls of powerful muskets and rifles were capable of punching through the wooden shields and killing the person on the other side. Open confrontation therefore became inadvisable, and instead stealth and speed became the keynotes for successful warmaking. These were tactical effects, but the introduction of firearms also had a strategic effect. For example, as we have seen, the Cree began purchasing firearms from the French and British in the seventeenth century, giving them an advantage in their territory. The nearby Assiniboine tribe, who at that time did not have access

to firearms, sensed that a strategic partnership was advisable, and so allied themselves with the Cree. In turn they received firearms, the Cree acting as an intermediary between the Europeans and the Assiniboine. Collectively the partners now embarked on a war against the Dakota (Sioux).

Already faced with the gun-toting Chippewa tribe, the Sioux were driven from the Great Lakes region by the hostile tribes, showing how firearms could alter balances of power that in some cases had existed for centuries. The Cree, Assiniboine and other gun-armed tribes met a more equal match in the form of the Blackfoot, who were also equipped with firearms. The consequence was much more costly engagements for all sides involved, both in terms of casualties and territory lost.

Of course, the acquisition of firearms by the Northern Native Americans also affected the conflict between Indian and settler, which became increasingly virulent as the rapacious settlers absorbed more and more land out west. By the end of the nineteenth century, furthermore, the United States was an established entity and the Federal Government was looking to use all its resources to remove Indian obstructions to the American land-grab. During the 1860s, for example, gold was discovered in Blackfoot territory, leading to a huge influx of prospectors and settlers. By this time, the Blackfoot were tremendously weakened anyway – the continuing destruction of the Plains buffalo by white hunters was not only eroding their wealth, but literally removing their source of sustenance and shelter.

The Matchlock

As firearms played such an important part in the evolution of Native American warfare, it is useful to explore the evolution of firearms technology between the seventeenth and the nineteenth centuries. During the sixteenth century, when the Native Americans first began to acquire guns, the matchlock arquebus left a great deal to be desired. The matchlock system worked via a smouldering slowmatch (lit prior to the engagement), which was held in a curved piece of metal known as a serpentine. When the trigger was pulled, the serpentine fell forwards under spring

power and dropped the match into an exposed pan of priming powder. The match detonated the priming powder, the consequent flame passed down a vent hole into the main chamber, where it ignited the principal powder charge to fire the gun. The loading process was slow, infuriatingly so in battle conditions as the shooter had to ram powder, wad and ball down the barrel, prime the pan with powder, blow on the match, and cock the serpentine, after which he could then actually aim and fire.

But this was not the end of the problems associated with the matchlock. They were shockingly inaccurate, with an effective range of about 25m (82ft). The need to keep powder and match dry for the gun to be

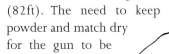

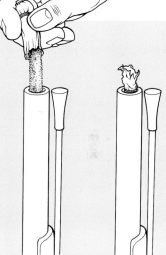

FIRING MECHANISMS
The four major firearms ignition systems of the pre-percussion age were: (A) Matchlock; (B) Wheellock; (C) Snaphance; (D) Flintlock. Native Americans were seen with all the types apart from wheellocks, which were expensive items to purchase even for Europeans, and were fragile when used in field conditions.

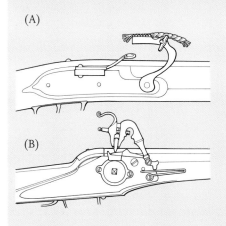

(A)

(B)

(C)

(D)

LOADING PROCEDURES
The muzzle-loading procedure began with tearing open a paper cartridge and pouring the power into the barrel, saving a small amount to prime the pan. The wad and ball were then rammed down onto the powder, the hammer cocked and the gun was ready to fire.

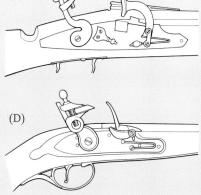

▲ An eighteenth-century flintlock musket. The musket appealed to the Native Americans not only because of the dramatic psychological effect of firing, but also because of its range and penetration, useful for both hunting and warfare.

effective presented serious difficulties during winter, or in the damp woodland conditions of the east and the north. The Indians understood this flaw, as the English explorer Henry Hudson discovered in 1607:

'The Salvadges [savages] perceiving so much, subtiley devised how they might put out the fire [the burning match] ... by which means they sawe they should be free from the danger of our mens pieces [guns] ... one of the salvadges came ... and taking the fier-brand which one of our company held in his hand ... he presently threw it into the water.'

Although there is some evidence of Indians using early firearms against settlers as early as the time of Hudson's experience, the matchlock arquebus probably impressed them more on account of its bang and smoke than its combat performance. Yet in time things would change. Beginning in the sixteenth century, the quality of gunpowder improved through the process of 'corning' – mixing the constituents with water and letting the mix dry into a large 'cake', which was then crumbled up into regularly sized granules. By achieving a more uniform mix of the ingredients, and providing air gaps between each granule of powder, 'corned' gunpowder burned faster and hence produced far greater levels of power, increasing the penetration provided and presented a more effective threat to Indian shields and armour.

The Flintlock

A more important innovation for the Indians, however, was the introduction of the flintlock, which entered firearms history around 1630. The flintlock did away with the need for a smouldering slowmatch. In its place came a spring locked 'cock' that gripped a piece

of flint. The gun was muzzle-loaded in much the same way as previous weapons, but when the trigger was pulled the cock dropped forward under spring pressure and the flint struck a steel set over the priming pan. The sparks created by the flint hitting the steel ignited the primer and fired the gun.

For the Indians, as for the Europeans, the flintlock had several far-reaching advantages over its predecessor. First, combined with the improvements in gunpowder, the flintlock was a more reliable weapon that was not susceptible to the vagaries of a smouldering match. The flint would, to a large extent,

▲ A group of Alaskan Indians, here seen photographed at the end of the nineteenth century, stand in front of totem poles. The warriors are armed with a mix of flintlock and percussion weapons.

work regardless of the weather, although there was still the need to keep powder dry. Furthermore, ignition was faster, and the knock-on effect was to make firearms more accurate, as there was less time for the shooter to wobble off target when he pulled the trigger. Flintlocks were also more practical propositions for both hunting and warfare because there was no glowing match to alert the prey or enemy. This was particularly important to the Indians, who conducted most of their hunting and warfare around daybreak, when light levels were still low and any bright object showed up clearly.

Finally, combined with the eventual standardization of firearms that accompanied the growth of mass armies, flintlocks became cheaper and more accessible to the Indians. In fact, on many occasions the colonizers issued edicts prohibiting the trading of weapons with the Native Americans. A British edict of 1641, for example, stated that: 'In trucking or trading with the Indians no man shall give them for any commodity of their, silver or gold, or any weapons of war, either guns or gunpowder, nor sword ... which might come to be used against ourselves.' Such restrictions had only a limited effect on the number of firearms in Indian hands. Rather, in many respects, the Indians eventually became known as useful gunsmiths, repairing lock mechanisms or using their superb woodworking skills to manufacture or mend stocks.

Because the Indian style of warfare preferred accuracy over volley firing, the Native Americans came to value high-quality weapons, although they purchased more than their fair share of 'trade guns'. These were cheap guns manufactured mostly for the Indian market, styled on French military muskets, albeit with reduced dimensions to cut the costs of production and transport. The firearms historian Carl Parcher Russell here describes the typical features of this type of gun:

▲ **An Indian buying weapons from settlers at the end of the eighteenth century; here he cautiously tests the flintlock mechanism. Settlers were more than willing to trade cheap guns for expensive furs.**

'The trade gun came from many different factories in Europe and the United States. Regardless of its point of origin, certain characteristics were constant. First of all, it was often light in weight, often short of barrel, and cheaply constructed. Commonly it was gauged to shoot a one-ounce ball; that is, it was sixteen-gauge, or about .66 caliber, although some were smaller. The trigger guard was clumsy in appearance and was large enough to permit access to the trigger even though the finger was enclosed in a glove or mitten. It was a gun made for the north country.

– *Parcher Russell* (1980)

Although trade guns were a little rough and ready, they were tailored to Indian requirements, particularly those Indians, as Parcher Russell points out, of the Northern territories. By being light and short they were more easily carried through the wilderness and more easily used from horseback, in the same manner as a cavalry carbine. The ability to shoot the gun while wearing a thick glove or mitten would also appeal to those Indians of the far north, who had to hunt or fight in the winter.

Rifles

Yet as we have seen, the Indian warrior also valued accuracy, and trade guns were not accurate – typical effective range would have been 50–100m (164–328ft), depending on the quality of the barrel, sights and ball. Far more appealing to the Native Americans was a decent quality rifle. Rifling consisted of spiral grooves cut into the bore of a weapon, these imparting gyroscopic spin to a projectile, dramatically improving its flight characteristics and therefore its accuracy and effective range. The European ancestry of rifling is much debated, but what is certain is that during the seventeenth century German gunmakers had perfected a short-barrelled flintlock rifle known to history as the Jäger rifle. This was a true hunter's weapon (their expense prohibiting widespread military use), relatively easy to carry in the field and capable of genuine accuracy out to 200m (656ft). German immigrants into Pennsylvania and Kentucky began producing their own local versions of the Jäger rifle, resulting in the famous 'Kentucky' or 'Pennsylvania' rifle of American lore.

RIEL'S REBELLIONS

The skills of both European and Indian warfare were combined in the Métis, persons of mixed French-Canadian and Indian ancestry who principally settled during the eighteenth century in Saskatchewan and Manitoba. The Métis lifestyle was a blend of cultures, mixing European-style agriculture with regular hunting and trapping expeditions, the latter involving the use of tipis for temporary housing.

RIEL'S REBELLIONS 1816–85

The Métis rebellions led by Louis Riel produced a string of battles along the Canadian border. Although the Métis won major battles at places such as Fish Creek, a series of defeats in 1885 brought the rebellion to an end.

Métis people relied heavily upon the fur trade for income, and hence came into conflict with the Hudson's Bay Company during the 1840s. The Company had a monopoly on fur trading in the area, and wanted to stop the Métis taking their goods to market in the United States. The outcome was a series of rebellions at first led by Louis Riel, a French-Ojibway businessman. The so-called 'Courthouse Rebellion' of 1849, a violent march on a courthouse in Fort Garry, began the protests, which were continued by Riel's son, Louis David Riel, from the late 1860s, when an influx of settlers threatened long-standing Métis land ownership. In 1869, Riel Jr and his 'border patrol' captured Fort Garry and by 1870 Riel had forced the Canadian government's hand, and was governor of his province. Yet Riel's political fortunes turned, and he was exiled in 1870, only returning in 1876.

The situation for the Métis worsened during the 1880s, when the Canadian-Pacific Railway began to cut through Métis territory and bring more settlers onto their land. In 1885, another Métis rebellion began, this time aided by an uprising of equally aggrieved Cree Indians. The scale of violence was far greater than previously. Cree warriors massacred nine settlers near Frog Lake, Saskatchewan, on 2 April and also defeated a Gatling-gun armed force of regulars at Cut Knife on 2 May. The Métis achieved their own victories, such as that at Fish Creek on 24 April, but the scale of Canadian forces soon proved overwhelming, with a serious defeat at Batoche on 9 May. With the Cree collapse at Loon Lake in June 1885, both the Cree and the Métis rebellion withered, and Riel was captured and hanged.

For the Indians who could obtain them, the Kentucky rifle was a superb hunting weapon that was incidentally perfectly suited to their sniping and ambushing style of warfare. Detailed accounts of the Northern Indian use of rifles are few and far between, but we catch some glimpses of their effectiveness. Published in 1839, Hugh Murray's *An historical and descriptive account of British America* describes the battles for Quebec that occurred during the Seven Years' War. In the following passage, he explains one of the failed attempts by the British to take Quebec in 1759:

'In 1759 preparations were made on a great scale for the conquest of Canada, comprising twenty sail of the line, with smaller vessels and transports, having on board 8000 veteran troops. These were placed under the direction of Wolfe, who was allowed the choice of all his officers. After a prosperous voyage the armament, on the 26th June, arrived off the Isle of Orleans. Quebec was defended by the Marquis de

▲ A dramatic reconstruction of the Riel Rebellions shows Canadian troops attacking Métis forces. Although the Métis had plenty of firearms, they faced troops armed with field artillery.

Montcalm, having under his command 13,000 men, of whom indeed only 2000 were regular troops, the rest being Canadian militia, with a few Indians. The attack having been long foreseen, full time was given him to entrench and strengthen his position ... Montcalm, strongly posted between Quebec and Montmorenci, poured in upon them a destructive fire; the Indian rifle told with fatal effect; and the assailants were finally repulsed with the loss of 182 killed and 650 wounded.'

– Murray (1839)

Although the account was written some years after the event, it is interesting that Murray highlights the role of the 'Indian rifle', in spite of the fact that the Native American element of Montcalm's force was small compared to his regular troops. Other accounts around this time bear out the respect that the settlers had for Northern Indian marksmanship. An article in *Wadie's Select Circulating Library*, published in Pennsylvania in 1833, describes the construction of a French fort at Detroit, the layout of the building obviously respecting the marksman who might watch from the surrounding woods:

'The fort of Detroit, as it was originally constructed by the French, stands in the middle of a common, or description of small prairie, bordered by woods, which were at that time untouched by the hand of civilisation. Erected at a distance of about half a mile [0.8km] from the banks of the river, which at that particular point are high and precipitous, it stood then just far enough from the woods that swept round it in a semicircular form to be secure from the rifle of the Indian.'

There is little doubt, therefore, that the settlers both feared and respected Northern Indians' capabilities with firearms. In the next chapter, we will continue our study of the Native American relationship with guns by looking at the percussion weapons of the nineteenth century, and how they affected the fight for the frontier. But at this point we need to venture further north and west, and see how the new ways of warfare affected the most isolated of the Native American tribes.

ARCTIC AND SUBARCTIC WARRIORS

The far reaches of North America contain some of the most inhospitable wildernesses in the world. In the subarctic and Arctic Circle, reaching from Alaska in the west to north-eastern Canada, the combination of sub-zero temperatures, bitterly cruel and long winters, frequently scarce food supplies and thin vegetation meant that only the hardiest of Native American tribes survived there. Yet survive they did. Tribes that inhabited these unforgiving lands included the Inuit, Kutchin, Hare and Yellowknife, plus several others. Nor did the austerity of their environment prevent the settlers from eventually moving up into their space. Contact between Alaskans and Siberians/Russians went back for millennia, but the European settlers also ventured far north.

FORT ST CHARLES
Fort St Charles, established by the French on the Canadian–US border in the eighteenth century, exemplifies the challenge the Native Americans faced when attacking settler fortifications. Cannon cover nearly every line of approach to the fort, and elevated firing platforms provided good fields of fire to infantry.

The Hudson's Bay Company was working up into the Arctic Circle by the eighteenth century, and the Klondike Gold Rush of the late nineteenth century drew more than 40,000 Americans up into Alaska and Canada. Yet the far Northern tribes of North America are a distinctive part of our study. Although they came into contact with the settlers, sometimes violently so, and adopted modern tools such as firearms, the isolation of many of the tribes meant that many of the older fighting methods were preserved for much longer than elsewhere.

Warrior Ethos

As well as fighting the climate, the far Northern Indians also spent a proportion of their time in minor warfare with each another, usually in brief but murderous clashes over issues such as fishing grounds or feuds. Because food was in such tight supply, the battles could be prosecuted with extreme focus, and casualties could be high. The warrior ethos was consequently high in such communities. Here Waldemar Bogoras, an ethnographer who studied the Chuchkee tribe of Siberia, here describes the inculcation of warrior values and skills in the young warrior. The study is relevant to this book because of

▲ **Indigenous Alaskan people outside the Hudson's Bay Company trading post at Fort Yukon. As well as desirable goods, the settlers also brought disease and alcohol to the Northern Native American tribes, slashing their numbers and weakening any armed resistance.**

the close cultural similarities and historical relationship between the Siberian aborigines and the Alaskan Native Americans:

'To be fit for fighting, every warrior undergoes hard training, and spends all his leisure in various exercises ... The hero must run for long distances, drawing a heavily-loaded sledge. He carries stone and timber, jumps up in the air, but above all, he fences with his long spear. He performs this exercise quite alone; and the chief feature of it is the brandishing of the spear with the utmost force, so that it bends like a piece of raw reindeer leg-skin. He also practices shooting with the bow, and uses for this purpose in various arrows, sharp and blunt. From all these exercises he acquires great skill and agility ... When he is shot at, he avoids the arrows by springing to one side, or parries them all with the butt-end of the spear, or simply catches them between his fingers and throws them back.'

— *Bogoras (1909)*

The account of this martial training evokes images of the Spartans of ancient Greece creating the perfect warrior, a potent mixture of raw physical power and skill at arms.

INUIT WARRIOR AND EQUIPMENT
This Inuit warrior is well equipped for Arctic hunting or warfare. The impressively sized snowshoes would give mobility over the deepest snow, while the rifle is wrapped in a fur-lined gun case (top right). The guncase was essential for stopping the gun mechanism getting wet then freezing solid.

Weapons and Armour

Two particular weapons are mentioned in Bogoras's account – the bow and the spear. Of the former, the wood available to the tribes of the far north was frequently unsuited to making self-bows, weakened as they were by constant damp or extremely cold temperatures. Many bows, therefore, were of the composite type, made from spruce driftwood enhanced by the addition of strips of bone, sinew or rawhide to improve their strength and elastic properties, and hence their power.

Adventurer John Murdoch, writing for *Popular Science* magazine in 1897, explained in detail the structure of the 'Eskimoo' bow during his trip into Alaska in 1891.

'As everyone knows, the Eskimoos, with very few exceptions, inhabit a region which is perfectly treeless, or at any rate where nothing grows but pines and spruces, whose soft, inelastic wood is entirely useless for making bows. They have overcome this difficulty very effectively by fastening along the back of the bow twisted cords of reindeer sinew in such a way that each cord is stretched when the bow is bent and flies back when the bow-string is released. As far as we know, no other race of savages makes use of this ingenious contrivance. Some tribes of Indians are in the habit of stiffening their bows by 'backing' them with strips of sinew, glued on, but the Eskimoo backing is made of cords and tied on.'

– Murdoch (1897)

Murdoch went on to observe that the power of these bows was actually formidable. Using arrows tipped with bone, flint or metal, the bow was, according to Murdoch, capable of being 'driven through the body of a polar bear' if there was no bone to obstruct its passage.

Murdoch's article is doubly interesting because it also reflects on the status of the bow in terms of its relation to the rifle, which by the late nineteenth century was part of Inuit life and warfare. He stated that every Inuit hunter 'had a pretty good rifle' despite 'a law against selling breech-loading arms and ammunition to "Indians"', a law he says 'was no better

◄ Sinew-backed Inuit bows carried formidable powers of range and penetration, the latter demonstrated by this large polar bear kill.

73–82m (80–90yd). Bearing in mind that in this period of history such range and accuracy outclassed many contemporary firearms, it is little wonder that the far Northern tribes retained their spears all the way into the twentieth century. Note also that the spear tips, made from iron or bone, were sometimes poisoned to improve their killing effect.

Apart from spears and bows, the Northern Indians fought each

enforced in Alaska than it was in old times on the plains'. Yet the poverty of the community meant that rifles were still beyond the means of many, hence bows remained important tools even beyond the period covered by this book.

Spears held an equal significance for the tribes of the far north, as they were integral to hunting large coastal or tundra animals such as caribou, seals, whales, deer and moose (plus humans, of course). While the atlatl spear-thrower noted in Chapter 1 may have had limited use in the woods of eastern North America, in the subarctic and Arctic zones it was an essential tool of hunting or warfare.

Observers of the Aleut tribe, which was concentrated in the far west of Alaska and in Siberia, noted in 1761 that the warriors could throw spears measuring up to 1.4m (4ft 6in) accurately to distances of

other with a wide range of other tools. Various types of club feature prominently, which were as much use for despatching injured animals as they were for combat. The clubs were either solid wooden weapons featuring ball-swellings at one end, or adze-type weapons featuring a sharp stone, metal or antler 'blade'. In addition to these, warriors also used bola missiles. These were made from lengths of rawhide with stones tied to each end, which were then thrown in a spinning motion. Originally bolas were devised to bring down running animals, principally by wrapping

► Inuits with spears hunt for fish in a river. The same spears could be applied in warfare, and were often thrown using atlatl launchers.

▲ An Inuit storage box plus two traditional weapons –
an axe consisting of a sharpened stone bound to a shaft,
and a 'knife' created from a piece of carved bone. Both
would be lethal when wielded with purpose.

the rawhide lengths around the legs, but they could do
likewise to running people, the stones causing severe
impact injuries while the rawhide could lacerate the
body as it wrapped round.

In response to this grim array of projectile and
stabbing weapons, it was common for the tribes of the
far north to wear some sort of body armour. This
came in some unique forms. In the Northern Pacific
area, we find examples of warriors wearing knee-
length suits of armour made from concentric rings of
thick hide sewn together. The design had a telescopic
effect, so the warrior could reach down and gather up
the lower rings if he wanted to leave his legs free for
running. Over this armour was a wide 'cape' made
from wood and sealskin, which literally formed a U-
shaped shield around the warrior's shoulders, upper
back and head.

More typically, the body armour of
the subarctic and Arctic tribes consisted
of bone, wood or walrus-ivory slats
sewn together in flexible plates and
hung over the shoulders, chest and
back. In some cases, matching arm-
guards or greaves provided protection
to the limbs. Material ingenuity
characterized Northern armour. In
some cases, armour was made by
coating a thick animal skin with glue,
to which stones and sand were stuck,
creating an extremely tough material.
Obviously such armour only had
limited effectiveness against the
increasingly effective firearms of the
period, but against clubs, arrows and
spears the protection afforded probably
could make the difference between life
and death.

Combat in the Frozen North

Although the scale of warfare in the far
North did not reach that experienced by the Eastern
and Plains Indians, on a local level it was brutally
enacted. David Jones has described a typical raiding
action by the Alaskan Kutchin warriors. As with Indian
tribes elsewhere, the Kutchin would often fight in
small raiding parties, typically in springtime when it
was easier to travel, but remaining ice still made it
possible to walk across rivers. The procedure for
organizing the attack was particularly ritualistic:

'Led by a band headman or a man known for his
prowess as a war leader, the raid would be instigated
by someone with the grievance. He or she notified the
potential war leader, who, in turn, selected three
subleaders. The family instigating the fight presented
the leader with a wolverine pelt, which he cut into
strips and gave to each man, who wrapped one around
his head. This act signifies his willingness to partake
in the action, as well as connecting him to the
wolverine, one of the most ferocious animals of the
subarctic forests.'

– Jones (2004)

Once assembled and embarked upon its raid, a war party, typically no more than 20 or 30 men strong, would descend upon the enemy village or camp at first light. In coordinated fashion, the raiders surged forward and attacked the enemy, using knives and spears to penetrate the skin of the tents, clubbing any who emerged or shooting down those who fled using bows or rifles. Mutilations of the bodies were common (it had ritualistic connotations of weakening the physical strength of the enemy), and Jones notes that all individuals in the camp – men, women and children – would be attacked.

Such a raid inspired a desire for revenge in the victims, and so led to decades of feuding between tribes that cost many lives. Edward Curtis' 1930 study of the Nunivak people of the Bering Strait paints a picture of equal brutality. A classic tactic was to surround the enemy cabins or tents, then bowmen would shoot into the habitations through the smoke holes. Those who were not immediately killed by these volleys had a naturally strong inclination to flee outside, where they were met by waiting Nunivak armed with clubs, spears and other weapons. All males were to be killed, while the women and children were taken as slaves or adopted into Nunivak families deprived of manpower by war. In return, the Nunivak were raided themselves. In one particularly ghastly

account, enemy Indians attacked a Nunivak village while the men were out hunting: 'They entered all the houses and killed the women and children. Some of the bodies they wrapped in sealskins and threw them into the fires [attacking Indians often torched the habitations]. Most of the children were hurled into the stagnant tundra water. The enemy tied throngs to the arms and legs of one old man and pulled him limb from limb' (Curtis, 1930). In retaliation, Nunivak warriors attacked the enemy camp, and killed everyone there.

The behaviour of the far Northern tribes does illustrate that Native Americans were capable, on occasions, of wars of annihilation against enemy tribes. Against the material depredations of the European settlers, however, they had little defence. European exploitation of whaling grounds, caribou herds and other natural resources, plus the introduction of fatal diseases, took a hideous toll on the Native Americans populations of the far north, and they consequently caused far fewer problems to settler expansion than the tribes of the Great Plains.

INUIT IVORY PLATE ARMOUR
Although it couldn't stop a bullet, this Inuit body armour would have had a good chance of stopping a spear or arrow strike. The panels of walrus ivory are lashed tightly together with cord, although not so tightly that the armour could not articulate around the wearer's body. Making such armour represented a considerable investment in time and effort.

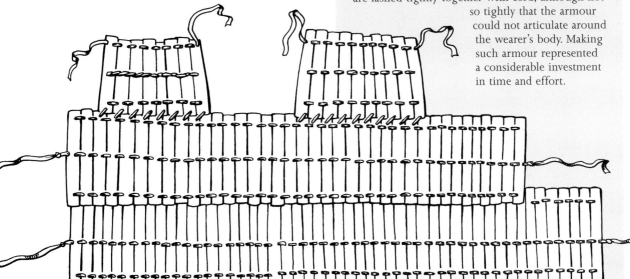

CHAPTER 3

Plains Tribes

From the Northern tribes covered in the previous chapter, we now swing dramatically south to encompass the Plains Indians, a blanket term for the tribes that extended from Alberta in Canada down to Texas in the southern United States, and from the Mississippi to the Rocky Mountains. As the term 'Plains Indians' suggests, the tribes of this chapter lived and died in a territory characterized by sweeping plains and prairies – what came to be called the 'big country'. The nature of this terrain, as we shall see, governed Plains warfare, particularly in relationship to the acquisition of the horse from the seventeenth century onwards.

One of the major Plains tribes, the Blackfoot, has already been studied in some depth in the previous chapter, although we will encounter it again here in various contexts. The great tribes of the wider cultural area included the Nez Perce, Cheyenne, Sioux (a blanket term incorporating the Lakota, Dakota and Nakota), Assiniboine, Plains Cree, Arapaho, Kiowa and Comanche. Yet

◄ A particularly epic representation of Custer's last stand, the American ranks being hacked down by attacking Plains Indians. Although highly dramatized, the painting captures the speed and aggression with which mounted Indians could attack.

NEZ PERCE WARRIOR
A mounted Nez Perce warrior, dressed for cold weather. In combat, his horse would be decorated with bright paints and symbols to inspire the warrior spirit in the animal. The Nez Perce tribe originally inhabited Idaho, southeastern Washington State and northeastern Oregon, and were pure hunter-gatherers.

while the history of the Northern tribes became, in part, intimately bound up with the history of Canada, south of the Canadian border (as it was established by the mid-1850s) the struggles and fate of the other Plains tribes was forged in the crucible of the expanding US frontier.

ROAD TO ALIENATION

Evidence of human presence on the western Plains dates back to 10,000 BC, and from that time until the intrusion of the Europeans, the Plains Indians lived in a timeless and largely nomadic fashion, hunting buffalo, fishing and periodically fighting wars among themselves. During the sixteenth century, Spanish settlers travelling up from Mexico and the South began to make contact with the southern Plains tribes, and, for reasons we shall explore, horses became available

▲ As the settlers pushed west, they became vulnerable to hit-and-run raids from the Plains Indians. Here some Indians put on an intimidatory show of force, while the settlers take cover behind their mounts.

to them from the Pueblo Indians, who in turn had acquired them from the Spanish. By the mid-eighteenth century, many of the Plains tribes were partially on horseback, while some (such as the Comanche) were entirely mounted.

Horses changed the face of Plains Indian society and warfare, but deeper changes were to come from the expanding American frontier. In 1803, the Louisiana Purchase brought vast swathes of central North America under US control, transferred from France, which was eager to fund its wars in Europe. The purchase made the western expansion of the American people inexorable, as they pushed out from the eastern United States into what seemed a limitless range of land. This expansion drove them directly into the territories of the Plains Indians, who even by the mid-1800s were still in control of huge territorial areas. Yet whereas many of the Eastern Indian tribes had capitulated to the settlers' growth by this time, the Plains Indians were ready for a fight.

▲ A Native American Plains warrior brings down a buffalo with a lance. Hunting buffalo required precise skills with the lance – the main target was through the shoulder, striking at the heart and other major organs.

The Slaughter of the Buffalo

There were two principal threats to the Plains Indian culture from the settlers. First, the settlers were voracious hunters, and began the steady process of slaughtering the North American buffalo herds on which the Plains Indians depended for their existence. Buffalo hides were used for clothing and for making tipis; buffalo meat was a major part of their diet, and the leftover bones were used for tools; and buffalo dung served as cooking fuel. Of course, the Indians themselves slaughtered buffalo in huge numbers, to support a total population that stood at around 239,000 people in 1872. Between 1872 and 1874, it is estimated that the Plains Indians killed around 1.2 million buffalo. Yet during the same period the settlers killed nearly 3.2 million animals, often just for the hide and sometimes just for sport. In fact, railway companies often allowed passengers to shoot buffalo from the carriages as the trains passed through the plains.

Furthermore, the wanton destruction of the buffalo appears to have been part of US strategy to clear the Indians from desirable lands. In 1874, Congress heard the testimony of Secretary of the Interior, Columbus Delano, who explained that 'The buffalo are disappearing rapidly, but not faster than I desire. I regard the destruction of such game as Indians subsist upon as facilitating the policy of the Government, of destroying their hunting habits, coercing them on reservations, and compelling them to begin to adopt the habits of civilization.' By the end

of the century, the buffalo herds of North America were essentially gone, reduced from millions of creatures to just a few hundred, saved at the last minute by Presidential reprieve.

Reservations

While the slaughter of the buffalo was underway, another piece of social engineering was being enacted against the Plains Indians. The Indian Removal Act of 1830 legislated that Eastern Indians were to be removed from desirable territories east of the Mississippi and resettled in other lands west of the river, thereby freeing up territories for the settlers. The act stipulated, among other clauses:

'Be it enacted by the Senate and House of Representatives of the United States of America, in Congress assembled, That it shall and may be lawful for the President of the United States to cause so much of any territory belonging to the United States, west of the river Mississippi, not included in any state or organized territory, and to which the Indian title has been extinguished, as he may judge necessary, to be divided into a suitable number of districts, for the reception of such tribes or nations of Indians as may

Nez Perce War 1877

The Nez Perce war was a brutal conflict resulting from settlers attempting to turn Nez Perce land over to cattle grazing. The Indians fought a long retreat to Montana, winning almost every battle along the way, before a final showdown at Bear Paw Mountain that forced their surrender.

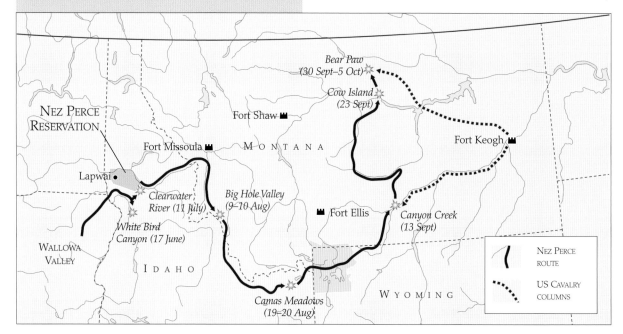

THE GRATTAN DEFEAT

In August 1854, a Lakota Indian killed a wandering cow in Wyoming. The Mormon owner of the cow, too afraid to go and look for it, reported that the Indians had stolen it, so 30 US soldiers under the command of Lieutenant John L. Grattan went to the Lakota village to forcibly reclaim the beast. The Indians were conciliatory at first, but they resisted Grattan's attempts to arrest their chief. In response, Grattan ordered his men to open fire, and the Indians retaliated – only one US soldier escaped alive. In consequence, the US government ordered a 600-strong force under General William S. Harney to take revenge, which they did by killing 85 Lakota and taking 70 women and children captive at the battle of Bluewater Creek in September 1885.

choose to exchange the lands where they now reside, and remove there; and to cause each of said districts to be so described by natural or artificial marks, as to be easily distinguished from every other.'

The language was legalistic and ordered, but the human fallout was traumatic and disastrous. The act resulted in conflict and expulsion, and drove Eastern tribes westwards towards the lands of the Plains Indians. By the mid-1850s, the Plains Indian themselves were targets of manipulative legislation, aiming to force them into reservations and allow settlers to utilize their land without recourse. The result was half a century of sporadic conflict, ranging from small-scale clashes to major wars. The Sioux Nation in particular fought regular wars with the US federal authorities from 1854 to 1890, the first war precipitated by a fabricated account that Lakota warriors had stolen a settler's cow (see 'The Grattan Defeat', above).

Officially, the US government often appeared to be seeking reasonable solutions, but in practice it allowed every treaty to be violated by the settlers, then took revenge against Plains tribes who took up arms to resist the intrusions. The Indian Wars saw four decades of atrocity and counter-atrocity, as well as the Federal forces suffering some substantial losses and defeats. For example, 800 settlers and soldiers died in the Minnesota Uprising of 1862, led

SIOUX WAR 1862

The Sioux War of 1862 consisted of a series of battles in Minnesota as the Plains Sioux attempted to expel the settlers from their territory. Up to 800 settlers were killed by the Indians, one of the highest civilian death tolls in US history, but they were eventually overwhelmed by US forces.

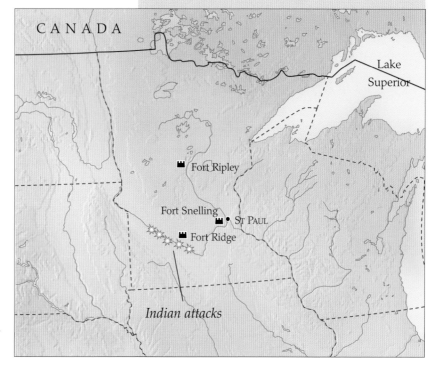

SIOUX CHIEF IN HEADDRESS
A Sioux chief is here seen in a full eagle feather war bonnet. The war bonnets
were not just items of impressive decoration, but the arrangements and types
of feathers used carried varying spiritual and military significance from tribe
to tribe. In Sioux culture, an eagle feather war bonnet was one of the
highest declarations of warrior skill, an item of clothing that carried
obligations to future courage as well as a testimony to past bravery.

by the Dakota chief Little Crow, and the US defeat at the Little Bighorn in 1876 has gone down as one of the most dramatic US military failures of the nineteenth century, outside of the Civil War.

Yet the end of the story is known – the Plains Indians ended up decimated and dispersed, their old way of life gone forever. Yet the reasons why they were able to keep the swelling force of the US Army on its toes for so long is the story of the remainder of this chapter.

HUNTING AND WARFARE IN THE PRE-HORSE AGE

As the horse revolutionized Plains Indian warfare so completely, it is worth considering how the Indians hunted and fought before this seminal change. Looking at the Plains Indians during the 1500s, however, shows up important continuities as well as contrasts. As we shall see, the Plains Indians developed long-standing techniques of hunting on foot that translated into mounted warfare from the seventeenth century onwards, and which were still used during the desperate wars of the nineteenth century.

What largely unified all the Plains Indian tribes was a culture that revolved around the rhythms and processes of buffalo hunting, a practice that had effects beyond mere subsistence activity. Indeed, the seasonal patterns of the buffalo – which dispersed into smaller groups in the winter when forage became scarce – affected tribal composition in a similar way. During the autumn and winter months, the tribe would often divide itself into smaller groups of families, these working as less-demanding hunting groups when compared to the full tribe. The lifestyle was largely nomadic, hence the tipi provided the ideal accommodation for the Plains Indians. In fact, a properly made tipi was windproof, waterproof, big enough for a decent-sized family and could be erected and dismantled in minutes by just two people.

When we look at the way the buffalo were actually hunted, we start to feel our way into the Plains Indian style of warfare. Buffalo are large, fast and dangerous animals, with an aggressive desire to protect their young, so intelligent, cooperative tactics were the root of Plains Indian hunting. When hunting small groups of buffalo, the basic technique involved simply stalking the animal from downwind, using cover and concealment to approach within bowshot. Sometimes the warriors would drape themselves in a wolf skin or other animal hide and crawl on all fours towards the target herd, the skin helping to both mask their scent and conceal their human appearance.

Tracking and Observation

A primary reason why so many Indians were employed as scouts by the US forces was their superlative skills in tracking and observation. By studying marks on trees and on the ground that were almost invisible to the untrained eye, an Indian scout could derive details such as how many men and horses had passed, whether some were injured or carrying weight and their direction of travel. They also had formidable powers of observation, as was attested by Edwin Denig, a fur trader in the 1850s who spent time with the Assiniboine:

STEALTH TACTICS
Two Indian scouts use animal skins to aid their observation of a US Army camp. Similar tactics were used during buffalo hunting, as the skins broke up the lines of the familiar human silhouette. There are accounts of Indians moving to within a few metres of settler soldiers while wearing such disguises.

'At a distance of 12 or 15 miles [19–24km] they will distinguish animals from timber, even supposing they are not in motion. If moving they will discern between horses and buffalo, elk and horses, antelope and men, a bear and a bull, or a wolf and a deer, etc. But the greatest mystery is how they make out anything living to be fair at such a distance, on the instant, when they themselves are in motion or the animal at rest. This they do when it is surrounded by a hundred other objects as like to living creatures as it is. Once pointed out, the movements are watched and its character thus determined. Their powers in this respect are truly astonishing and must be acquired. They also judge very correctly of the relative distances of objects either by the eye or to each other. Smoke can be seen rising on the plains at a distance of 60 miles, and they will tell from that or a lesser distance within a few miles of the place where it rises.'

– *Denig* (1930)

Such tactics were fine for small numbers of animals, but a massive herd required far more dramatic strategies. There were two essential methods of hunting large buffalo herds on foot. The 'piskin' involved the hunters forming themselves into a long 'V' shape, the tip of the V terminating in either an enclosure or a sheer drop or escarpment. The hunters would channel the buffalo

herd between them, startling it into a stampede that was funnelled down the V towards the enclosure, where they would be trapped, or fall off the edge of the escarpment. The second method, known as the 'surround', is fairly self-explanatory – the hunters would form themselves around the herd in a large circle, then tighten the circle around the prey, shooting into the mass of panicking creatures with arrows and lances. This strategy involved greater risk of death and injury at the horns of a fear-demented buffalo, but it was also a test of the hunter's bravery and stamina, and doubtless provided good fireside stories.

THE HORSE

More than anything, it was the acquisition of the horse that changed the nature of Plains Indian hunting and warfare. Horses gave unprecedented mobility and

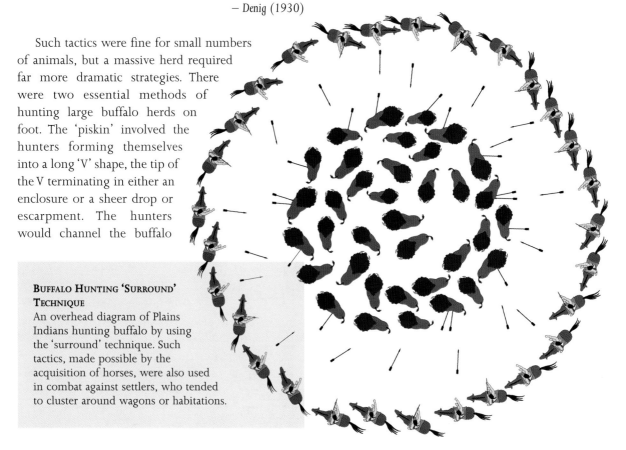

BUFFALO HUNTING 'SURROUND' TECHNIQUE
An overhead diagram of Plains Indians hunting buffalo by using the 'surround' technique. Such tactics, made possible by the acquisition of horses, were also used in combat against settlers, who tended to cluster around wagons or habitations.

▲ **A Native American man hunting buffalo on horseback, 1853. The ability to shoot and reload the bow from horseback gave Native Americans a distinct combat advantage against settlers armed with flintlock firearms.**

speed, access to more distant territories and opportunities to develop new styles of warfare. The Plains Indians acquired horses during the seventeenth and eighteenth centuries. First contact with horses came to the Pueblo Indians through their relationship with the Spanish (see box feature, overleaf), but steadily horse ownership spread through the southern Plains, aided by the 1680 Pueblo revolt, which saw the transfer of thousands of Mexican horses to the Plains Indians. By the mid-1700s, horse ownership had spread as far north as the Blackfoot tribe.

The Native Americans were almost preternaturally gifted horsemen. John Irving, writing in the 1830s, here recounts the subjugation of a mustang at the hands of a Plains Indian:

'A young Indian first came forward, and led up a bright, jet-black mare; after him followed another, holding in his hand a long buffalo tug, or halter, which restrained the wild motions of a two years' old colt … At one moment he dashed swiftly around at the full stretch of the long tug which secured him – then pausing, and shaking his long mane over his head, he fixed the gaze of his almost bursting eyes upon his captor. Then raising his head, and casting a long, lingering, and almost despairing gaze upon the hills of the prairie, which till then had been his home, he

PUEBLO INDIANS

The Pueblo Indians, an ancient Native American tribe inhabiting what is today New Mexico and Arizona, had lived for centuries in the Southern territories before making contact with the Spanish during the late sixteenth century. 'Pueblo' comes from the Spanish word for 'town', the Spanish applying the label on account of the structural similarity of Pueblo Indian settlements to Spanish towns. They struck up a precarious relationship with their new European neighbours, hiring out their labour for work on Spanish settlements or farms.

▲ An adobe Pueblo settlement. Adobe consists of sand, clay and water, plus an additional fibrous material, and was shaped into dried bricks.

Spanish attempts to convert the Pueblo to Catholicism, however, helped precipitate the Pueblo Rebellion of 1680–92, led by the Indian chief with the rather ironic (given the cause of the rebellion) name of Popé. The rebellion at first brought success for the Pueblo. They ejected the Spanish from Santa Fe, killing 400 of them, and largely drove the Spanish from the territory. Although the Pueblo then successfully resisted Spanish attempts at counter-attack, the integrity of the resistance was steadily undermined by Popé, who alienated himself from his people by dictatorial behaviour. The rebellion progressively collapsed from within and, by 1696, the Spanish had reclaimed the territory they had lost.

made a desperate leap forward, dragging to the ground the Indian who held the end of his halter. Others, however, rushed to his assistance, and held him in. The crowd then attempted to close round him, but he reared upon his hind legs, and kept them at bay with rapid and powerful blows of his fore feet. At length a young Indian who was standing near, threw off his robe and crept cautiously towards the animal from behind. With a sudden leap he bounded upon his back, and seized the tug, which was secured in his mouth. Before this, the efforts of the animal had been violent; but when he felt the burden upon his back – when he felt the curbing hand of his rider – he sent up a shrill and almost frantic scream – he bounded in the air like a wild cat – he reared, he plunged, but in vain. His rider was a master hand, and retained his seat as unmoved as if he had constituted part of the animal itself. He curbed him in – he lashed him with his

◀ A Cheyenne Indian on horseback. The introduction of the horse into Plains Indian culture not only provided a new vehicle of warfare, but dramatically increased the scale of tribal hunting territories.

heavy whip, until he crouched like a dog upon the prairie. His spirit was crushed; and the last spark of freedom was extinguished. Shortly after, one of the hunters came up and tied a pack upon his back. He made no resistance, and they led him off with the rest, to finish his days in drudgery and toil.'

— Irving (1835)

Such accounts of Indian horsemanship are far from uncommon. Realizing the potential of the horse, the Plains Indians instructed their youth in horsemanship from the earliest age. Richard Hook notes that in the Comanche 'both boys and girls were capable riders by the age of seven' and that a virtual big-top repertoire of trick riding skills were standard talents, such as the ability to lean out from a galloping horse and snatch a person or other object from the floor. When hunting buffalo on horseback, the hunters, mounted on the swiftest 'buffalo-runner' mounts, could now run down selected prey, shooting them from horseback with either a bow or a gun. The same could apply to warfare, the horse giving the Indians the ability to move at speed around their enemies, disorientating them and providing targets of opportunity.

Mounted Warfare

Until the nineteenth century, the bow was the most common weapon of the mounted Plains Indian; its rate of fire was higher than that of early firearms, and it was more convenient to load and shoot on a jolting horse than a muzzle-loading musket. Nevertheless, there are plenty of accounts of Indians who did master handling flintlock firearms from horseback. An article in the *Literary Gazette*, dated 1836, provides an account of the life of Blackbird (c.1750–1800), chief of the Omaha Indians, whose territory was traditionally in modern-day South Dakota, Nebraska and Kansas. Blackbird was true warrior, and the article describes a perfect fusion of horse and gun:

'In attacking a Kanza village, he rode singly round it, loading and discharging his rifle at the inhabitants as he galloped past them. He kept up in war the same idea of mysterious and supernatural power. At one time, when pursuing a war party by their tracks across the prairies, he repeatedly discharged his rifle into the prints made by their feet and by the hoofs of their horses, assuring his followers that he would thereby cripple the

CROW INDIAN HORSE
A Crow Indian horse in full regalia, including bridle, reins (braided rawhide), saddle (wooden frame covered in rawhide) and stirrups. The pendant hanging over the centre of the horse's forehead, made from cloth and beads, represents the Morning Star.

▲ **A striking photograph of Crow Indians, all armed with long lances. The lance was originally a buffalo hunting tool, but was easily adapted to warfare.**

Indian agent Jos M. Street to the US Secretary of War, Lewis Cass, explains the friction between the Sioux Indians and the neighbouring Sac and Fox. In one incident, the writer explains, three Sac Indians were out hunting when they spotted intruders in their territory:

'They [the Sacs] say they were only three in company, and perceived two Sioux in a prairie within the limits of the Sac and Fox lands hunting buffalo. One of the Sacs went towards the Sioux with professions of friendship, but the Sioux threw their blankets and breast cloths off, and shot him. The other two Sacs (who had been concealed from the Sioux), immediately pursued them, and killed both Sioux. They also say that they had no war party.'

– Street (1831)

fugitives, so that they would easily be overtaken. He, in fact, did overtake them, and destroyed them almost to a man; and his victory was considered miraculous by friend and foe.'

Allowing for some mythologizing, it was undoubted that the equal enthusiasm of Indians for guns and horses would have produced many talented firearms-equipped mounted warriors. This talent reached its peak of perfection during the nineteenth century, when fixed cartridge revolvers and magazine-fed rifles made the process of reloading on horseback that much simpler, and dramatically increased rates of fire (see below for a more extended discussion of percussion weapons).

The acquisition of horses in many ways actually increased the likelihood of armed conflict for the Plains Indians. Horse raiding of the type described in Chapter 2 became a major cause of localized armed conflict. Furthermore, horses enabled tribal warriors to venture further afield in search of buffalo and other food, and in so doing raised the possibility of coming into contact with similarly roaming hunters from other tribes. In fact, this possibility of previously unlikely contact with other tribes often became reality. A US government document from 1831, written by

Such a local action was, as the writer implies in the document, just part of a general pattern of clashes emerging between the Sioux and the Sac and Fox tribes in the early 1830s. In balance to the episode just described, he goes on to explain a similar incident in which the Sac and Fox are the intruders:

'Four Sioux were hunting in a prairie, near the head of the Terre Bleu river, at a place called by the Indians 'the Hill that stands up', about 70 or 80 miles [112–128km] north of the line of the land sold to the United States at Prairie des Chiens last year. They were surprised by ten Sacs or Foxes coming rapidly and unexpectedly upon them. The Sioux fled, and the Sacs fired and killed two of them. The remaining two Sioux turned, fired and killed one Sac or Fox, and effected their escape to the nearest encampment of Sioux.'

– Street (1831)

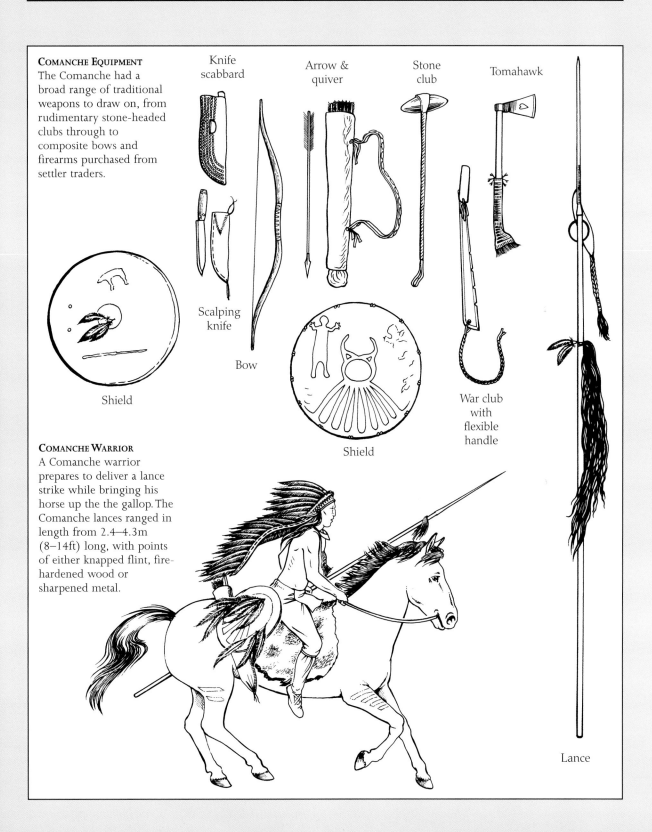

COMANCHE EQUIPMENT
The Comanche had a broad range of traditional weapons to draw on, from rudimentary stone-headed clubs through to composite bows and firearms purchased from settler traders.

Knife scabbard

Arrow & quiver

Stone club

Tomahawk

Scalping knife

Shield

Bow

Shield

War club with flexible handle

COMANCHE WARRIOR
A Comanche warrior prepares to deliver a lance strike while bringing his horse up the the gallop. The Comanche lances ranged in length from 2.4–4.3m (8–14ft) long, with points of either knapped flint, fire-hardened wood or sharpened metal.

Lance

A significant feature of this quotation is the reference to 'land sold to the United States'. Although such conflicts were intertribal, they were often intensified by the territorial dislocation caused by settler expansion and US land negotiations with the Native Americans. Street acknowledges this fact, and gives Cass a cautionary message regarding the Sioux state of mind:

'Major Taliaferro has no doubt fully apprised you of the state of feeling in which he left the Sioux, and the course it indicated, if left to themselves. To me, recently, they hold language like this: "The treaty of 1830 [the Indian Removal Act of 1830] has been broken. Our land has been invaded and our people killed while quietly hunting meat for their families. We want satisfaction. Our fathers at Prairie des Chiens told us, if we were struck, not to revenge it; but to leave it to our great father the President, and he would see justice done us. We tell you now, that we will be quiet until the waters flow again in the spring. Then if our great father does not see justice done to us, we will wait no longer. We will revenge our brother warriors."'

– *Street (1831)*

WAR HORSES

Much like human warriors, Native American horses were also highly decorated to show their performance and status as warhorses, and to channel the spirits and powers on which the Indians relied. The painting was performed by the *Tsunkan-wakan* (Holy Horse) medicine man using red and white clay paint, and some of the classic symbols were as follows:

SYMBOL	MEANING
Antelope horns	Power, speed
Dragonfly	Protection
Representation of wounds	Illustrated places the horse had been wounded in battle
Outline of a man on horse's chest	Signified the horse had ridden down an enemy in battle
Zigzags down legs	Evoked the fear of the lightning spirit

The explicit threat made by the Sioux was, as we have seen, ultimately realized in decades of bitter warfare between the Plains Indians and the US Army. For tribes whose very existence was based upon buffalo hunting, and whose use of horses gave them access to vast swathes of the land, any policy that ate into land ownership was bound to cause trouble.

WEAPONS OF THE PLAINS INDIANS
Firearms

The Plains Indians, as with all the other Indian tribes studied in this book, were both beneficiaries and victims of firearms. This dual relationship with firepower was at no time more apparent than during the nineteenth century, when firearm design underwent several critical revolutions. In the second decade of the century came the invention of the percussion cap. This cap – a small brass cup filled with fulminate of mercury – rendered the flintlock system obsolete (although flintlocks remained in use for many years thereafter). Instead of a flint striking a steel above a pan of loose priming powder, the percussion cap system worked simply by placing the cap on a nipple under a hammer. When the trigger was pulled, the hammer dropped on the cap, detonating the fulminate of mercury through impact, and the resulting hot flame flashed down a vent in the nipple into the main chamber, igniting the main charge and firing the gun. Percussion weapons were more reliable and produced faster lock times (the time between pulling the trigger and the gun firing) than flintlocks.

Alongside a whole new generation of percussion long guns, the percussion system also led to the creation of true revolvers. By the 1830s, the firearms legend, Samuel Colt, was producing his first percussion-cap revolver, a five-shot handgun that, once loaded, could fire as quickly as the user could cock the hammer and pull the trigger. By the end of the Civil War in 1865, the United States was a land awash with handguns.

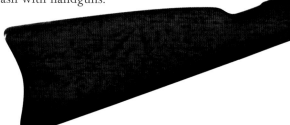

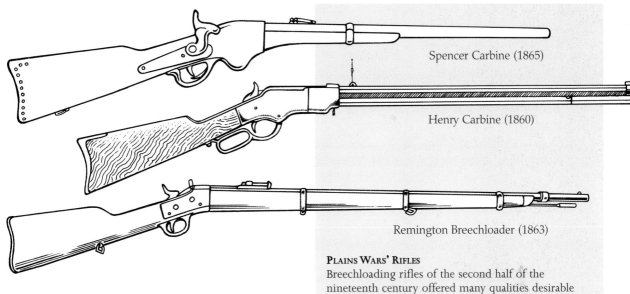

Spencer Carbine (1865)

Henry Carbine (1860)

Remington Breechloader (1863)

PLAINS WARS' RIFLES
Breechloading rifles of the second half of the nineteenth century offered many qualities desirable to the Plains Indians. They had practical ranges of hundreds of metres, for example, and could be reloaded from horseback. The biggest problem was obtaining adequate supplies of ammunition.

But even greater changes were to come. The percussion cap was superseded during the first half of the nineteenth century by the fixed cartridge, the system in which primer, powder and bullet were combined in a brass case. Space does not allow us to explore the full implications of the fixed metal cartridge, but its most important achievements were the dramatic acceleration of reloading times (particularly once allied to magazine feed), the perfection of breech-loading firearms (that ultimately offered more power than muzzle-loaders and made rifling a standard feature) and greatly improved reliability – there was no more loose powder to become damp or spilt.

By the time of the American Civil War, therefore, the world of firearms had been utterly transformed. For the Plains Indians, of most interest were the big 'buffalo hunting guns', such as the powerful Sharps,

Spencer, Springfield and Henry/Winchester rifles. The latter is a good example, albeit at the end of our period, to show how far firearms had come since the beginning of the century. Chambered in powerful big-game hunting calibres (such as .45-75 and .50-95 Express), the Winchester Model 1876, for example, could drop a buffalo or enemy accurately at several hundred metres and was fed from an 11-round underbarrel tubular magazine – all the operator had to do to reload was to cycle the lever attached to the trigger guard.

Yet Native Americans were essentially at the end of the firearms supply chain, acquiring often suspect

▲ **An 1873 Springfield trapdoor carbine. With its powerful .45-calibre round, the Springfield could kill buffalo and humans with ease. It was used both for and against the Plains Indians, and was wielded by figures such as the great Geronimo.**

quality firearms directly through trade, or taking weapons during raids and battles against the settlers. A problem that was never overcome, even in the age of fixed cartridges, was that of ammunition supply. The Plains Indians were excellent at maintaining and repairing their weapons, showing material ingenuity – broken stocks, for example, could be repaired with strips of rawhide.

They also treated their firearms as more than simple violent tools; many Indian rifles are decorated with brass studs along the woodwork, showing their status as aesthetic objects. Obtaining ammunition, however, was a constant problem, which probably accounts for the fact that although most Plains Indian warriors had acquired rifles by the 1870s, at the battle

▼ **Plains Indians circle and attack a wagon train. For the settlers under such an attack, the best defence was to huddle together and put out withering fire from behind the wagons. A warrior party would typically break off the action once it had suffered a handful of casualties.**

of the Little Bighorn in 1876 only around 30 or 40 per cent of the Native Americans involved in the battle actually used them in combat, the rest relying on their traditional weapons. Ammunition supply must have been complicated by the fact that one tribe would have multiple types of weapon. After the Little Bighorn, a study of cartridge cases at the site revealed that the Indians had used Henry, Winchester, Springfield, Remington and Sharps rifles, as opposed to the Springfield carbines and Colt revolvers issued to the Federal troops.

Plains Indians were generally slower to adopt handguns, at least as practical hunting and combat tools, because bows largely outclassed them in terms of performance. Yet handguns became increasingly common Indian side-arms following the American Civil War, when a glut of military-surplus weapons flooded the market. Illuminating our study of Plains Indians and firearms is a story from Charles S. Bryant, who in 1864 recounted the experience of Minnesota

▲ **A Native American-owned Sharps rifle. Plains Indians often decorated the stocks and fore-ends of their rifles, typically with brass studs or, as shown here, decorative animal-skin slips. In proficient hands, the Sharps had a rate of fire of around ten shots per minute.**

soldiers and settlers battling with hostile Sioux warriors. In one instance, Sioux warriors attacked a settler outpost, and two men began what seemed a very personal sniper duel:

'As an instance of the manner in which the fight was now conducted, we would mention a part of the personal adventures of Mr. Walter P. Hills, a citizen, who three times came as a messenger from the fort during the time it was in a state of siege. He had just returned to the post with dispatches from this office,

the evening before the attack was made. He took part in the engagement, and killed his Indian in the early portion of the fight, before the enemy was driven across the river.

He afterward took position at one of the port-holes, where he paired off with a particular Sioux warrior, posted behind a tree of his own selection. He, being acquainted with the language to a considerable extent, saluted and conversed with his antagonist, and as the opportunity was presented, each would fire at the other. This was kept up for about an hour, without damage to either party, when the Indian attempted to change his position, so as to open fire from the opposite side of his tree from that which he had been using hitherto. In this maneuver he made an unfortunate exposure of his person in the direction of the upper bastion of the fort. The report of a rifle from that point was heard, and the Indian was seen to make a sudden start backward, when a second and third shot followed in rapid succession, and Mr. Hills beheld his polite opponent stretched a corpse upon the ground.'
– Bryant (1864)

The style of battle between these two men is reminiscent of the stylized bow fights seen in early chapters – the two men speak with each other over the course of the hour-long shootout, occasionally letting off shots from behind cover. In classic Indian style, the Sioux warrior shoots from behind a tree, understanding that even the most powerful contemporary rifle would be unable to penetrate a substantial tree trunk. In fact, it is only his decision to change position, plus the exceptional marksmanship of his opponent, that results in his demise.

▲ A photographic portrait of a Crow chief in war paint. He carries a typical Plains Indian self-bow, of short dimensions and made from a single piece of wood.

The Bow

However ingrained firearms became in Plains Indian society, the bow endured to the end of our period. Jim Hamm, an expert on the Native American bow, here explains the Plains Indian bow for mounted warriors:

'In the Plains area horsemen prevailed, and their bows were normally shorter than those used by Indian who hunted on foot (with the exception of the sinew-backed yew bows). The Plains bows were usually 50" [127cm], or shorter, and the handy, maneuverable weapons were ideally developed for horseback hunting or warfare. Rectangular in cross section, with the widest part of the bow being at the handle, most bows were 1" [2.5cm] to 1¼" [3cm] wide at the handle and about ¾" [1.9cm] wide at the tips. In pre-Columbian, pre-horse days the Plains bows were longer, and 55–60" [140–152cm], and comparable to bows used by historical foot Indians.'

– *Hamm (1989)*

FIRING FROM HORSEBACK
Firing a bow and arrow from horseback not only required experience to judge the right moment of release, it also needed perfect balance on the part of the rider. Mounted shots were typically taken at close to medium range, the rider allowing the horse to take him up to the target before drawing and firing in one swift movement.

Hamm illustrates how the introduction of the horse changed the nature of bow construction. Prior to the horse, when most hunting and warfare was done on foot, bows were longer and more powerful, necessary for shooting at buffalo at long range. Once the Plains Indian warrior was mounted, however, bows had to be more compact, but any reduction in power was compensated by the ability to get closer to prey on horseback. In terms of the wood for the bows, chokecherry, wild plum, hickory, ash or crab apple were typical, backed with sinew. Arrowheads were, in earlier times, made from flint, but by the time of the Little Bighorn battle they were almost exclusively made from iron, which was easier to fashion into shape and more durable while fighting.

The power of the Plains Indian bow was not to be doubted. A contemporary observation of the bow in action during a hunting expedition leaves no doubt as to its power as a weapon (see quotation, right). Such performance may relate to the longer, more powerful bows of the Plains Indians, but there is little doubt that whatever the design they would have been capable of serious and lethal penetration.

'HE CARRIED A BOW AS LONG AS HE WAS TALL, WITH ARROWS OF PROPORTIONAL LENGTH, WITH WHICH HE COULD KILL GAME A HUNDRED YARDS [91M] DISTANCE. I KNEW AN INSTANCE OF THE TERRIBLE FORCE OF THESE ARROWS WHICH IS WORTHY OF NOTE. AIMED AT THE BEAR, THREE YEARS OLD, BUT HAD TAKEN REFUGE IN THE TOP OF A TREE, IT WENT THROUGH THE BRUTE'S BODY AND WAS PROPELLED FORTY OR FIFTY YARDS [37–46M] BEYOND.'

– NEWCOMBE (1978)

more compact, these shields measuring 0.5–0.6m (1ft 8in–2ft) in diameter. Both historians and contemporaries have argued over the efficacy of such shields in relation to musket balls and rifle bullets. The percolated conclusion of the arguments is that the shields were capable of stopping a bullet from a low-velocity weapon, such as a handgun at long range, but against any powerful firearm they gave little protection. For the Indians who carried them, however, their efficacy was only partly bound up with their physical qualities. The 'medicine' attached to the shield was equally if not more important. Like the war paint decorating warrior and horse, similar motifs were painted on shields, or they were hung with guardian elements such as feathers or animal claws. Great ritual and care was taken while preparing such shields. Richard Hook notes that:

'Shields were prevented from touching the ground, and kept on tripods facing the sun to renew their power. The belief in the shield's spiritual power was such that sometimes only the thin protective cover, a miniature of the shield or a lacework shield were actually carried into battle.'

– Hook (1985)

Other Weapons

Alongside the bow, the Plains Indians carried the typical assortment of clubs, trade knives, tomahawks and spears that we have seen in other chapters. They also carried shields and basic armour. Regarding the shields, the pre-horse communities produced shields of several layers of buffalo hide, heat shrunk and hardened with glue made from buffalo hooves, sometimes padded with feathers, fur or other projectile-absorbing material. A typical shield would have measured around 1m (3ft 4in) in diameter, but mounted warriors required something far

Plains Indian armour was also produced from animal hides, often arranged in a double thickness with sand between the layers. Yet by the nineteenth century, by which time most of the Plains tribes had witnessed the reality of firearms penetration, such armour had largely been discarded and the warrior would ride into battle in his soft clothing.

WARRIOR SOCIETY

Although the Plains Indian tribes never replicated the hierarchical intricacies of European armies, this is not

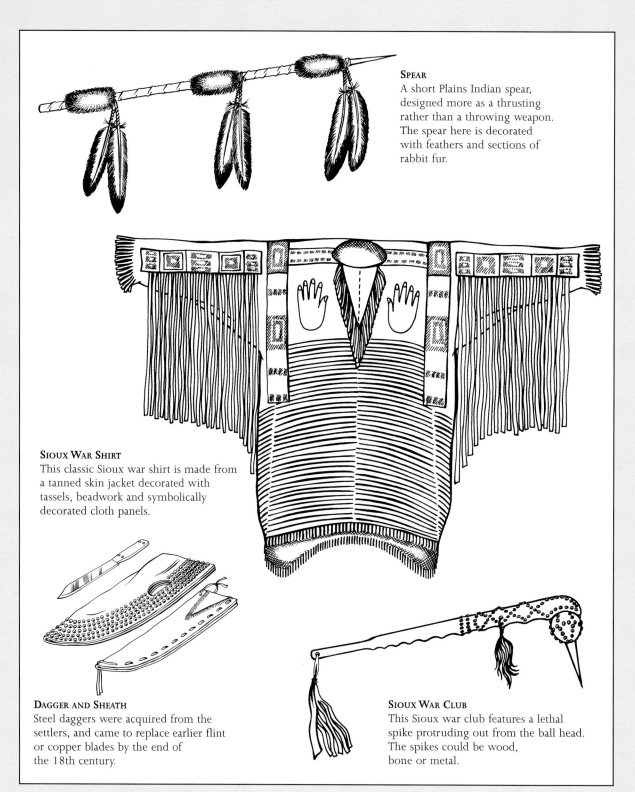

SPEAR
A short Plains Indian spear, designed more as a thrusting rather than a throwing weapon. The spear here is decorated with feathers and sections of rabbit fur.

SIOUX WAR SHIRT
This classic Sioux war shirt is made from a tanned skin jacket decorated with tassels, beadwork and symbolically decorated cloth panels.

DAGGER AND SHEATH
Steel daggers were acquired from the settlers, and came to replace earlier flint or copper blades by the end of the 18th century.

SIOUX WAR CLUB
This Sioux war club features a lethal spike protruding out from the ball head. The spikes could be wood, bone or metal.

▲ Sioux warriors on horseback in war bonnets, and carrying lances and shields. In combat, lances were sometimes thrown or used as hand-held weapons in a manner similar to European cavalry.

to say that they did not have their own rank systems. Each tribe would be headed by its chiefs, of which historian Richard Hook notes two fundamental divisions:

'While the structure of each tribe's authorities was complex, the most general distinction between leaders was that between the war chief and civil chief. The civil chiefs were generally senior, older men, concerned with the day to day life of the tribe; while war chiefs – the officers of the warrior societies – were vigorously involved in martial affairs.'

– Hook (1985)

Hook goes on to point out that the 'idea of the Plains Indian chiefs as autocrats is mythical', demonstrating that they held their positions largely on a consensual basis, noting that 'a poor chief would soon lose his position, while the band of a popular leader would prosper, and expand' (Hook, 1985). The meritocratic nature of Plains Indian

▲ A group of Plains Indians perform a war dance in full war outfit, brandishing flintlock muskets, stone-headed war clubs, spears and tomahawks. War dances could be performed both before and after combat.

leadership is important, for it goes some way to explaining the efficacy of Plains Indian resistance to the settlers. Furthermore, good warriors were highly respected throughout Plains Indian society, having influence in the tribe's council – a group of chiefs and elders who made major tribal decisions – as well as inspiring up-and-coming young men with the virtues of being a warrior.

Tribes also divided themselves into distinct warrior societies, these serving as both social and military clubs with their own rites, rituals, clothing and customs, and which served to give them status amongst the mass population of the tribe. Some tribes, such as the Blackfoot, Kiowa, Mandan and Arapaho, had a further complicated system for grading warriors within the society. The system for progressing up the ranks was a mixture of purchase, seniority and experience. Those at the bottom of the ladder – boys just coming to fighting age – bought their way into the lowest grade of warriors by offering gifts to those above. If their gifts were accepted, there was a ritual initiation and feast and the boys entered the warrior society, while those who had sold them membership attempted to buy themselves into the next grade. Unlike the British system of purchase, however, warriors had to demonstrate skill and courage in battle

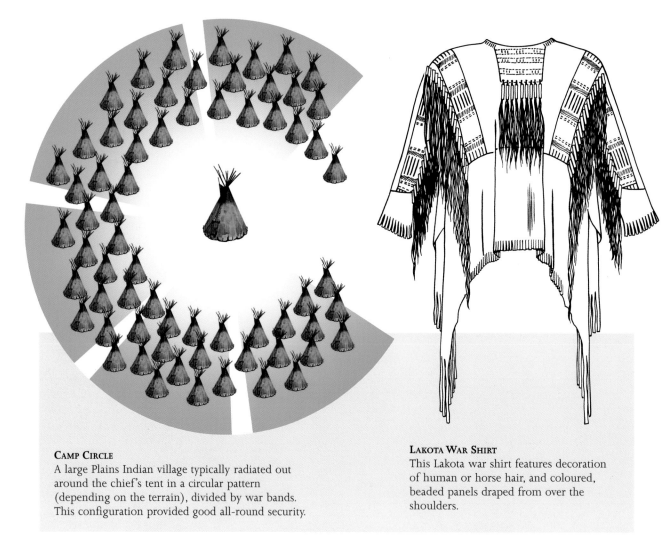

CAMP CIRCLE
A large Plains Indian village typically radiated out around the chief's tent in a circular pattern (depending on the terrain), divided by war bands. This configuration provided good all-round security.

LAKOTA WAR SHIRT
This Lakota war shirt features decoration of human or horse hair, and coloured, beaded panels draped from over the shoulders.

before they were allowed to step up in grade, the ultimate objective being to reach the top warrior grade in the tribe before retiring.

Not all of the Plains Indian tribes followed such systems, however. The Crow, Sioux, Cheyenne, Assiniboine, Pawnee and Arikara were all 'non-graded' societies (see Hook, 1985, for a full discussion of the workings of Plains Indian warrior societies). Here there was a nominal equality between the warriors, although much like a star international soccer player, a well-experienced and highly regarded warrior would be the object of other societies' envy, and they would attempt to attract him away from his existing society with gifts.

The societies were fiercely competitive, even abducting wives from their rivals, and demonstrating absurd bravery on the field of battle in attempt to raise the fame and notoriety of their own group. Hook notes, however, that being a highly regarded warrior was a double-edged sword: it conferred status and

▲ **An impressive photograph of a Sioux family in full dress. By the time this photograph was taken, in the late nineteenth century, the Sioux had largely been confined to reservations after defeat in the Indian Wars.**

respect, but there were also obligations to keep showing near-reckless courage on the battlefield, often resulting in being injured or killed by enemy action.

Women

A little-studied aspect of Plains Indian society, at least in terms of its warrior culture, is the role of women. Some of the existing studies note that there is evidence of women joining Sioux war parties or raids, although the visual depictions tend to show women acting as baggage carriers for the fighting men.

Yet not all Indian women simply went along in a supporting role. Several Plains Indian women became respected horse raiders, such as the Crow Indian Woman Chief and Running Eagle of the Piegan tribe. The fact was that Plains Indian women were just as

◀ **Chief Bigfoot was a Lakota Sioux chief, and was one of the Sioux warriors most feared by the settlers. A diplomat as well as a soldier, he was finally caught and killed in the infamous Wounded Knee massacre (1890).**

capable on horseback as any man, and the choice to be a female warrior was seen as unusual rather than an aberration. Furthermore, in bitter inter-tribal wars, and in the conflicts against the settlers, women and children were just as much targets as combatants. This became painfully apparent during the second half of the nineteenth century, when Federal troops began what virtually amounted to a policy of extermination against certain noncompliant tribes.

A particularly notorious example is the 'Wounded Knee Massacre', which occurred on 29 December 1890. The context of the massacre was the rise of the Ghost Dance religion amongst the starving and dispossessed Lakota Indians in South Dakota. One of the tenets of the new religion was the disappearance of

TRANSPORT
Transporting weighty supplies was a challenge for mounted warriors, but the nomadic lifestyle of many Plains Indians taught them how to adapt simple natural materials to perform heavy tasks. Here two long, flexible boughs are formed into an A-frame carriage for a bundle of supplies, the rear tips of the boughs bevelled to act as slides over rough ground. Personal supplies were also carried in small pouches worn on the hip.

▲ **A disturbing image of some of the Native American dead from the Wounded Knee Massacre in 1890. The Indians were killed by US Army artillery and rifle fire, and the dead included 44 women and 16 children.**

the settlers, so naturally the US Government became nervous that the reservation Indians might revolt. A US clampdown resulted in sporadic violence and the arrest of some Lakota leaders. Many of the Ghost Dance adherents now saw resistance as futile, including the Miniconjou chief Big Foot, who gathered 350 individuals around him and took them to the Pine Ridge Reservation in South Dakota, but they were forced by US troops to camp at the nearby Wounded Knee Creek. A large force of the US 7th Cavalry, 500 strong, promptly surrounded the camp, and even established artillery positions overlooking the native tipis.

On 29 December, as the US troops attempted to disarm the Indians, a scuffle broke out and a rifle discharged. It was the cue for a massacre. The US troops opened up with their rifles and artillery and by the time the firing stopped up

to 300 Indians were dead, a significant proportion of them women and children.

Such massacres were far from uncommon during the nineteenth century, and they proved that the idea of non-combatants was redundant. Therefore it is not unreasonable to understand how we hear of Indian women picking up rifles and fighting back – their own survival, and that of their children, was at stake.

PLAINS BATTLES

The nineteenth-century geographer and ethnologist Henry Rowe Schoolcraft observed how closely tied Plains Indian tactics could be to wide open spaces. Here he quotes one Lieutenant Pike, who makes

MAJOR ENGAGEMENTS: PLAINS WAR 1820–90

As this map illustrates, the entire High Plains area of
the United States experienced major engagements
between the settlers and the Native Americans. The
cause of the Plains Wars was largely a matter of
simple demographics – by 1870 there were about
40 million settlers in the United States, many of
whom were pushing against the 300,000 Plains
Indians in pursuit of agricultural land and buffalo
hunting. Despite the Indians' generally superior
warrior skills, they could not stop being swamped
by sheer numbers.

observations on the contrasting tactics of the
Chippewa and Sioux Indians:

'The Sioux attack with impetuosity; the others
defend with every necessary precaution. But the
superior number of the Sioux, would have enabled
them to have annihilated the Chippeways long since,
had it not been for the nature of their country, which
entirely precludes the possibility of an attack on
horseback. Also it gives them a decided advantage over
an enemy, who, being half armed with arrows, the
least twig of a bush turns the shaft of death out of its
direction. Whereas, the whizzing bullet holds its
course, nor spends its force short of its destined

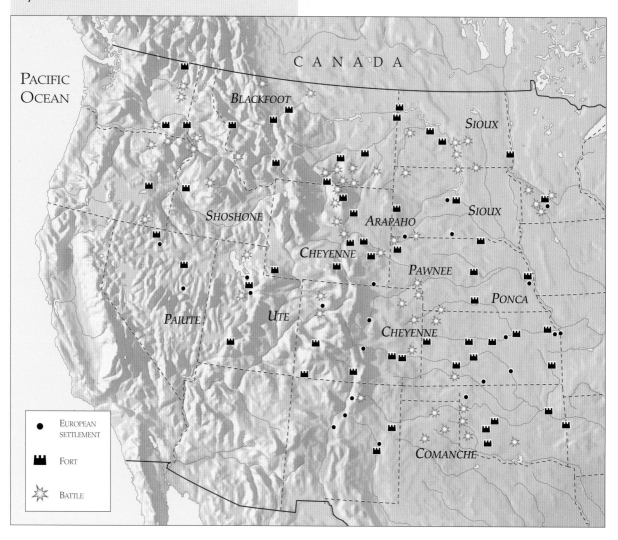

PACIFIC
OCEAN

CANADA

BLACKFOOT

SIOUX

SHOSHONE

SIOUX

ARAPAHO

CHEYENNE

PAWNEE

PONCA

PAIUTE   UTE

CHEYENNE

COMANCHE

●   EUROPEAN
     SETTLEMENT

🏰   FORT

✶   BATTLE

▲ US cavalry and Plains Indians make an exchange of rifle fire from horseback. Although the settlers had many talented horsemen, the Indians took warrior horsemanship to near perfection.

victim. Thus, we generally have found, that when engaged in a prairie, the Sioux came off victorious; but if in the woods, even, if not obliged to retreat, the carcasses of their slaughtered brethren shew how dearly they purchase the victory.'

— *Schoolcraft* (1821)

Lieutenant Pike observes that familiarity with the terrain could be a constraint as well as an advantage. The Plains Sioux, according to Pike, lost the advantage of mounted warfare once they ventured off the prairie and into the woodland, the converse being true for the Chippewas. His view is not universally applicable across all the Sioux, since there were tribes that inhabited woodland and forest areas, and doubtless these were just as comfortable fighting in those environments as any other woodland tribe. Yet the

plains and prairies undoubtedly required a unique set of skills to master in war, particularly in the fields of navigation and communication across such vast expanses of open ground.

In terms of navigation, an intimate knowledge of the local and regional terrain was of course built into the Plains Indian warriors from childhood. Settlers (those on friendly terms with the Indians, of course) would sometimes obtain charcoal-sketched maps of surrounding territory, often finding these more accurate, or at least useful, than the maps produced by European cartographers.

Edwin Denig, a fur trader operating around Assiniboine territory in the 1850s, explained in one account that the chief had drawn him a map encompassing 'a circumference of 1,500 miles' and that 'so correct was the drawing that we had no difficulty in finding their camp the following winter in deep snow, one month's travel from this place' (Denig, 1930).

Of course, when maps based on local knowledge couldn't help, the Plains Indians relied upon ancient skills of navigation, such as reading the prevailing wind direction or navigating by the stars or the position of the sun. Migration patterns of animals, or the flight paths of birds, would often indicate the direction of water.

FETTERMAN DEFEAT 1866

In 1866, in an act of bravado, Captain William J. Fetterman set off with 80 men, declaring that he could ride straight through Sioux territory with impunity. Following a party of Indian decoys, Fetterman went deep into Sioux territory before being ambushed at the later-named Ambush Hill and his party massacred to a man.

While travelling, particularly during a warlike expedition, the members of a war party also had to communicate with one another to convey intentions to those in distant sight or out of visual range. Such communication was particularly important between the scouts out front and the main war party following behind. Each war party would agree, or understand, a system of signalling. Ground messages were commonly used, these consisting of patterns of twigs and stones arranged on the ground. The warriors created V-shaped arrangements of materials, for instance, to indicate the direction of travel taken by the lead party, and different coloured stones or pieces of charcoal would denote features, such as rivers, hills and camps.

Apart from ground signals, the Plains Indians also used a variety of distance signals. Horsemen would ride in distinctive patterns, which would convey a message to their comrades observing them from afar. Signallers bounced sunlight off pieces of mirror or

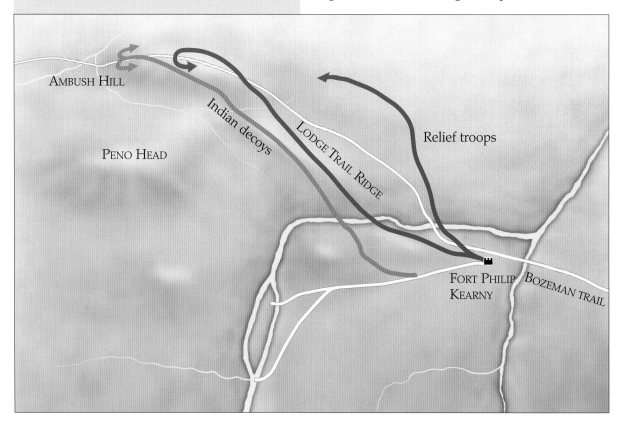

AMBUSH HILL

PENO HEAD

Indian decoys

LODGE TRAIL RIDGE

Relief troops

FORT PHILIP KEARNY

BOZEMAN TRAIL

polished metal. Smoke signals were another option, these being used to both provide information and to coordinate separate forces. Washington Irving, writing about explorations amongst the Crow people, explains how smoke was used as a communication system:

'The travellers [the settlers] kept on their way due east, over a chain of hills. The recent rencontre showed them that they were now in a land of danger, subject to the wide roamings of a predacious tribe; nor in fact, had they gone many miles, before they beheld sights calculated to inspire anxiety and alarm. From the summits of some of the loftiest mountains, in different directions, columns of smoke began to rise. These they concluded to be signals made by the runners of the Crow chieftain, to summon the stragglers of his band, so as to pursue them with greater force. Signals of this kind, made by outrunners from one central point, will rouse a wide circuit of the mountains in a wonderfully short space of time; and bring the straggling hunters and warriors to the standard of their chieftain.'

– *Irving (1836)*

▲ **A party of Native American US Army Scouts track across the Plains. The US Army used Indian scouts owing to their superior field skills, particularly when it came to tracking.**

Here the Crow Indians used smoke as a tool of centralized command, gathering different groups of warriors to the chief while also alerting them to a potential threat or target.

The Plains Indian skills at navigating, signalling, horsemanship and all aspects of warfare would be sorely tested during the nineteenth century, when they came up against their greatest foe – European settlers and the US military machine. Whether battling Texas Rangers, US cavalry or infantry, or just civilian settlers and traders, the Indians quickly realized that they had come up against a formidable opponent. While the settlers lacked many of the field skills on which the Plains Indians relied, they compensated with mental and physical toughness, skill with firearms (particularly in the case of civilian hunters) and their sheer numbers. When the two sides met in battle, therefore, the outcome was generally uncompromising and bloody.

Here we shall make a close study of two major Plains Indian battles – the battle of Adobe Walls in 1874, and the infamous battle of the Little Bighorn in 1876. Interestingly, these battles not only demonstrate traditional Plains Indian warrior tactics, but also the incorporation of some European military skills, illustrating that the Native Americans were open to learning from their opponents.

The Battle of Adobe Walls

The context for the battle of Adobe Walls was mounting tension between the Native Americans and the settler buffalo hunters. In the period following the Civil War, the situation for the Plains Tribes regarding

▼ A US Cavalry scouting party stop to recce an Indian village. While the soldier uses binoculars to scan the village, the Indian relies on naked eyesight – Indian scouts were known for their exceptional vision.

the buffalo worsened considerably. Buffalo-hide clothing reached new levels of fashionability in the heavily populated Eastern territories, resulting in thousands of hunters flocking west armed with rifles. The result, as we have seen, was a massacre of the buffalo. At one point, a local store at the hunters' settlement of Adobe Walls, built around an abandoned fort in the Texas Panhandle, was receiving about 1000 buffalo hides every day. The situation was made even more critical by the development of a new tanning process that made the buffalo's thin summer coat just as useful to the settlers as the long winter coat. In short, the settler hunters could kill all year round including during the breeding season. For the Comanche people, the time to act had come.

In mid-1874, the Comanche chiefs Quanah Parker and Spotted Pony arranged a meeting with Kiowa, Arapaho and Cheyenne chiefs to discuss the situation. In an impassioned debate, the tribal chiefs agreed that only violent resistance was going to stop the wholesale

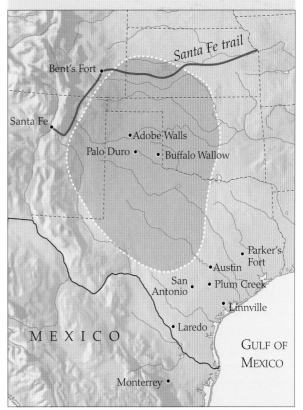

◀ Quanah Parker was a famous Comanche leader, the son of a Comanche father and a European mother. An accomplished warrior, Parker died of natural causes in 1901, and his funeral was attended by 1500 people.

equipped with revolvers. Furthermore, the hunters had plenty of cover in their buildings. The hunters' habitations were constructed out of a mix of logs and sod, materials that in the right density can easily stop any bullet.

In classic style, the Indians attacked in full force, streaming down towards the settlement in full war

COMANCHE TERRITORY 1860

The Comanche tribe's territory in the southern Plains meant that they were well-placed for raiding operations into Mexico and Texas. Although by the mid 1870s most Comanche were confined to reservations, their more skilful diplomacy meant they retained something of their traditional life.

slaughter of the buffalo. It was decided that Adobe Walls had to fall.

On one level, the advantage seemed distinctly in the Indians' favour. The combined Indian war party that rode out towards Adobe Walls at dawn on 27 June 1874 numbered up to 700 warriors, whereas Adobe Walls contained merely 28 buffalo hunters and a handful of other civilian residents. Yet the hunters did have some advantages. First, they were well armed with Sharps and Remington buffalo guns, most in .44 and .50 calibres and all capable of dropping horse or rider at a considerable distance. Ammunition was plentiful – the local Rath & Co. store had more than 11,000 rounds available – and each hunter was also

◀ At the battle of Adobe Walls in 1874, Comanche, Cheyenne, Kiowa and Arapaho Indians attacked a buffalo hunters' settlement in Texas. Although the battle saw the deaths of three settlers, the Indians sustained 15 deaths from accurate rifle fire, and finally broke off the attack.

hunters, fine marksmen all, selecting their targets and hitting them at several hundred metres. The Indians replied with volleys of fire, only to see them disappointingly absorbed by the hunters' buildings. Yet the battle of Adobe Walls was not just an exchange of rifle fire. Many Indians dismounted and moved in close among the buildings, emptying their revolvers and rifles through any gaps in the structure of the houses. The only way they could kill the hunters, however, was actually to enter the dwellings and fight at close quarters, but when they presented themselves at windows and doors they were shot down by the hunters' revolvers.

paint with lances, guns and bows at the ready, screaming their war cries. Two settlers who had been asleep in a wagon were shot and scalped, then the war party descended on the houses, circling around them as if they were so many buffalo.

After such a ferocious start, the battle steadily turned against the Indians. Horses and warriors began to drop from heavy-calibre rifle rounds, the buffalo

During the battle, the Indians applied some tactics that were derived from service in the US Army, as Douglas V. Meed in his book *Comanche 1800–74* relates:

'Uniquely, the warriors put some army tactics into practice. Warriors attacked, circled the buildings shooting, and then at a bugle call, fell back and regrouped. When the bugler blew the charge, they attacked again. Years later, Quanah would recount that the bugler was an army deserter who had joined the tribe. Wearing war paint and a feathered bonnet, he blew army bugle calls to direct the fighting.'

— *Meed* (2003)

Although the bugler in this case was an army deserter, the fact that Quanah integrated the tactic into his battle plan is significant. It shows that the Plains Indians learned some new techniques of battlefield coordination from the settler armies. Ironically, in this case the temporary withdrawals may have done more harm than good. By pulling back and gathering together, the Indians would have formed a good target for the hunters' long-range rifles, unless they managed to place themselves behind significant cover.

The Battle of Adobe Walls ultimately deteriorated into one of attrition for the Native American attackers. Although three buffalo hunters were killed

SCALPING

The origins of scalping are unknown, but it appears to have arisen among some (but not all) Native American tribes during the eighteenth century. For many Indian tribes, the scalp was regarded as holding a person's spirit, hence to lose a scalp was a shameful event, while to gain one produced a sense of victory – some celebrations following a successful scalping action could last for days, even weeks. Once collected, scalps were used in various ways according to tribal traditions. Often they were applied as decoration, hung from weapons, shields, clothing, horses, tipis and so on, visually demonstrating the power and victories of a particular warrior or society.

The actual techniques of scalping varied slightly. Some scalps consisted of a small portion of hair and skin cut around the crown of the head, whereas in other cases the incision ran in a circle from the forehead to the back of the head, leaving the victim virtually with an exposed upper skull. In most cases, a scalped individual would be dead, killed in earlier fighting, but scalping was also performed while the victims were still alive.

▲ **An engraving imagines the last acts of the Fetterman Massacre, 1866, with Indian warriors cutting the scalps from both the dead and the living, and brandishing them as signs of victory.**

▲ **On 29 November 1864, a 700-strong party of the Colorado Territory Militia attacked a Cheyenne and Arapaho camp, killing 133 Indians, many of them women and children.**

during the action, some two dozen Indians were dead and many more wounded, including Quanah Parker. In the end, the attack was broken off and the demoralized Indian force returned home. Worse still, the Adobe Walls action provoked the US Government to launch a major campaign against the southern Plains tribes, which became known as the Red River War (1874–75). Over the course of a year of fighting, the Southern tribes were effectively ground down into small scattered parties, desperately fighting for survival.

The Battle of the Little Bighorn

Adobe Walls shows how vulnerable the Plains Indians were when fighting an emplaced and sharpshooting enemy – in effect, they struggled to fight against an enemy who fought as they sometimes did. Against conventional forces, however, the battle could be tipped in their favour, especially if the opposing commanders made serious errors of judgment, such as in the case of the famous US cavalry commander Lieutenant Colonel George Armstrong Custer, in the battle known in US history as Little Bighorn.

The US wars to control the belligerent Sioux Indians had been rumbling on and off since the mid-1850s, and they would reignite in 1876. The source of contention this time was the Black Hills in Dakota, a region placed in the Great Sioux Reservation by the Fort Laramie Treaty of 1868. However, during the 1870s pressure built on the US Government to buy back the Black Hills to aid railroad development and prospecting. Settlers exploring the Black Hills had frequently met violent and understandable xenophobia from the Lakota, who also took to raiding non-Indian settlements, and the US government was moved to deliver a simple choice to the Indians – hand

over the Black Hills, or face military action. It came down to the latter.

In the spring of 1876, US forces under the command of General Philip Henry Sheridan set out in what they hoped would be a decisive action against the Lakota and their allies, the northern Cheyenne. There were three columns deployed, the aim being to trap the opposing Indians in a pincer movement. A 'Montana column' (450 men) under Colonel John Gibbon set out from Fort Ellis, Montana, while General Alfred H. Terry led a column of 925 men from Fort Abraham Lincoln. Terry's column included the 7th Cavalry under the command of the headstrong Custer. Another column of 1000 men, headed by General George Crook, left Fort Fetterman in May.

Terry and Gibbon were guided to their target – a major Lakota encampment on the Little Bighorn River – by the able guidance of allied Crow scouts. A plan was formed, which in essence involved Custer, with some 700

US SEVENTH CAVALRYMAN
Forged in civil war, the cavalryman returning to the western plains after 1865 was a better-equipped and better-led combatant than the Sioux had driven from the Bozeman Trail just a few years before. This sergeant carries a breech-loading carbine firing a 405-grain soft lead bullet with tremendous range and stopping power. His issue Colt revolver is reliable and rugged, if slow to load. Cartridges for both at this time could be carried in a hand-stitched cartridge belt or the more traditional cartridge box on the trooper's belt.

cavalry, attacking the camp from the south, driving the occupants against Gibbon's men descending from the north. Custer was given some leeway to modify the plan according to contingencies, which he duly did by altering the route of approach to the Lakota camp and, on 25 June, splitting his forces into three main components: a scouting party of 115 men under Captain Frederick W. Benteen; three columns of troops commanded by Major Marcus Reno; and five columns of troops under his own command. While Reno moved directly at the southern end of the village, Custer took his force up the Little Bighorn, hoping to attack the Cheyenne part of the encampment from further north. Yet as Reno neared the Sioux tipis, a group of Lakota warriors sounded the alarm and the battle began.

The battle of the Little Bighorn has been well-documented from the US side but an excellent account of the battle from the Lakota point of view comes from Chief Red Horse, whose testimony was contained in the 10th *Annual Report of the Bureau of American Ethnology* (1893). History notes that when Custer's men attacked the Indian camp, they had underestimated the numbers of Indians present, which may have been as great as 6000 warriors, although about 3000 is a more likely figure. Custer had around 800 men in his force. Yet notwithstanding the superiority in manpower, the shock of the US attack was still profound:

'The day was hot. In a short time the soldiers [Reno's battalion] charged the camp. The soldiers came

BATTLE OF THE LITTLE BIGHORN 1876

This map shows the (likely) lines followed by Custer and the other US cavalry soldiers during the Battle of the Little Bighorn. Custer seriously misjudged the strength and the positions of the Native American warriors he faced, and allowed himself to be outflanked and then surrounded. Driven into confined terrain, the final battle for his survival lasted for about an hour, but resulted in the complete destruction of his force. At least 280 US soldiers lost their lives in the action.

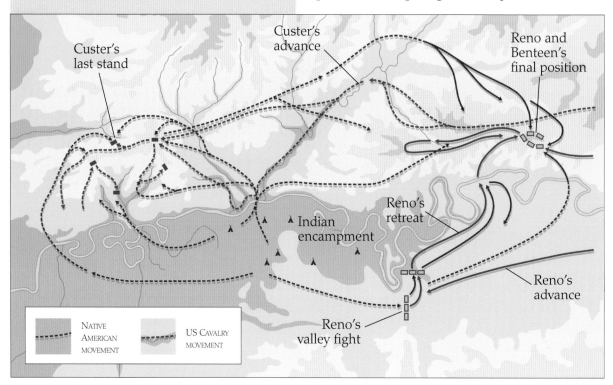

Custer's last stand

Custer's advance

Reno and Benteen's final position

Reno's retreat

Indian encampment

Reno's advance

Reno's valley fight

NATIVE AMERICAN MOVEMENT

US CAVALRY MOVEMENT

on the trail made by the Sioux camp in moving, and crossed the Little Bighorn river above where the Sioux crossed, and attacked the lodges of the Uncpapas, farthest up the river. The women and children ran down the Little Bighorn river a short distance into a ravine. The soldiers set fire to the lodges. All the Sioux now charged the soldiers and drove them in confusion across the Little Bighorn river, which was very rapid, and several soldiers were drowned in it. On a hill the soldiers stopped and the Sioux surrounded them. A Sioux man came and said that a different party of Soldiers had all the women and children prisoners. Like a whirlwind the word went around, and the Sioux all heard it and left the soldiers on the hill and went quickly to save the women and children.'

– *Red Horse* (1893)

The defeat of Reno's attack was a critical early victory in the battle. Although initially thrown into confusion, the Indians responded well, counter-attacking with mounted troops who managed to outflank Reno's forces, which had been deployed in a defensive line. Once the Indians were confident that Reno was not going to come back at them (he had lost half his command in this engagement), they turned their attention to Custer's troops on the other side of the Little Bighorn. An assault across the river by Chief Gall of the Hunkapa band pushed Custer's men further northwest, driving them onto a high ridge, while other Cheyenne and Sioux bands joined in the attack from other directions. Red Horse's account of the battle gives a vivid portrayal of Custer's defence:

'... the Sioux charged the different soldiers [Red Horse uses the word 'different' to denote Custer's men, as opposed to Reno's] below, and drive them in confusion; these soldiers became foolish, many throwing away their guns and raising their hands, saying, "Sioux, pity us; take us prisoners." The Sioux did not take a single soldier prisoner, but killed all of them; none were left alive for even a few minutes. These different soldiers discharged their guns but little. I took a gun and two belts off two dead soldiers; out of one belt two cartridges were gone, out of the other five.

◀ **Sitting Bull was a famous Lakota Sioux holy man and warrior. He was a key figure in the defeat of Custer at the Little Bighorn, and a general focal point for Sioux resistance.**

The Sioux took the guns and cartridges off the dead soldiers and went to the hill on which the soldiers were, surrounded and fought them with the guns and cartridges of the dead soldiers. Had the soldiers not divided I think they would have killed many Sioux. The different soldiers [i.e. Custer's detachment] that the Sioux killed made five brave stands. Once the Sioux charged right in the midst of the different soldiers and scattered them all, fighting among the soldiers hand to hand.

One band of soldiers was in rear of the Sioux. When this band of soldiers charged, the Sioux fell back, and the Sioux and the soldiers stood facing each other. Then all the Sioux became brave and charged the soldiers. The Sioux went but a short distance before they separated and surrounded the soldiers. I could see the officers riding in front of the soldiers and hear them shooting. Now the Sioux had many killed. The soldiers killed 136 and wounded 160 Sioux. The Sioux killed all these different soldiers in the ravine.'

– *Red Horse* (1893)

There is little sense of organized tactics on the part of the Indians here, purely opportunistic attacks and an aggressive determination to overwhelm the disorganized US command.

CROW SCOUT
This Crow Indian Scout, a member of the US 7th Cavalry, wears a mixture of traditional Native American and regular US Army clothing (a military issue Army four-button jacket). The unorthodox dress indicates that this warrior probably dates to the early 1870s, for after 1876 Indian scouts were issued with full military dress. He is armed with the redoubtable Springfield 1873 carbine, a .45-calibre weapon that had a muzzle velocity of 411m/s (1350ft/s) and a range of more than 1000m (3280ft).

Red Horse does hint at the fact that had Custer's command been unified in its defence then the battle might have turned out differently. At one point in the battle, some Indians even dressed in the uniforms of dead US soldiers, adding to the confusion of the US troops.

Custer's defeat was complete within about an hour. Of more than 200 men that Custer took above the Little Bighorn River, not one survived. Custer himself

was found with two bullets in him, the one to his head probably added port-mortem. Following this action, the Indians sought to capitalize on their victory by pursuing Reno and Benteen, but the arrival of the rest of the US forces put them to flight.

The defeat at the Little Bighorn illustrates the fact that complacency among the enemy often featured in Plains Indian victories, indeed victories amongst any Indian peoples. Speedy horsemanship and the ability to travel fast on foot meant that the Indians could quickly take advantage of any tactical sloppiness, and such was the case at Little Bighorn.

▶ **Major-General George Armstrong Custer performed poorly during his training as an officer cadet at West Point, and showed confused leadership skills during his final battle at the Little Bighorn. This photograph dates from the Civil War, where he distinguished himself as a impetuous cavalry commander.**

▼ **Indians with Winchesters chase panicked US troopers in the sketchbook of Sioux warrior Amos Bad Heart Buffalo, who served as a US Army Scout. His drawings represent an Oglala Sioux's record of the wars that ended his tribe's traditional way of living.**

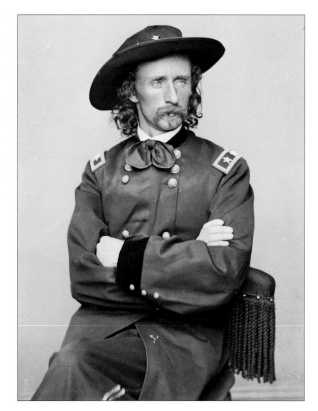

CHAPTER 4

Southwestern Tribes

The Apache and Navajo are justifiably some of the most enduring Native American tribal names in popular memory. Their resistance, and that of several other Southwestern tribes, to the encroachments of the settlers endured well into the late nineteenth century, and can be attributed to a martial spirit and formidable warrior skills.

Most histories of Native American tribes have a sad inevitability about them. So far in this book, we have seen the typical pattern emerge of Indian resistance to the encroaching settlers gradually giving way to subjugation or even destruction. Yet the case of the tribes of the American southwest, the Apaches being the most famous, is particularly pitiable. Here we see the Native Americans trapped between the forces of Spain and Mexico to the south and the United States from the east, the friction between Indians and settlers spiralling into grotesque wars in which extermination of the native peoples was often a cornerstone of settler policy. In balance, however, the Indians

◀ **Apache warriors retreat at full gallop following a horse-raiding mission. Back at their camp, the fresh horses acquired during the raid would be distributed equitably among the tribal members.**

of the southwest were particularly tenacious foes, with warriors skills that took a heavy toll on their enemies right until the very end of the nineteenth century.

The geographical focus of this chapter is essentially on what is today Arizona, Colorado, Mexico, New Mexico and western Texas. This area incorporated many Native American tribes less well-known to history, including the Zuni, Keres, Piri and Tiwa, but is principally remembered for one of the most legendary of all Indian peoples – the Apaches (to which the equally famous Navajo were related). While, therefore, this chapter will focus heavily on Apache history and warfare, it will also use this great tribe to illuminate the practices of others, such as the Hopi and the Mohave.

▲ A poignant photograph of a Pueblo Indian, illustrating the simplicity of dress for which they were known. The Pueblo had to adjust to Spanish, Mexican and American rule.

APACHE RESISTANCE

The Apaches were not a single tribe, but rather, like the Algonquian of the northeastern United States, a body of linguistically related peoples scattered over a fairly wide range of territory. The principal Apache groupings were the Western, Navajo, Chiricahua, Jicarilla, Kiowa, Lipan and Mescalero, these inhabiting (by the early 1800s) pockets of territory that reached from central Arizona across to the Pecos River in Texas and north to the headwaters of the San Juan River in Colorado. Geographically, the Apache territories varied considerably, from mountains and plains through to arid, inhospitable deserts. The more northerly Apache tribes managed to avoid settler intrusions for some time into the sixteenth century, but for the tribes in the south, blood was soon spilled as they came into contact with the belligerent Spanish.

The Spanish Wars

By the 1540s, Spanish *conquistadors* were making incursions across the Mexican border and up the Rio Grande river, clashing with the Chiricahua and Mescalero Apaches as they went. The colony of New Mexico was established by the 1590s, and its first governor, Juan de Onate, largely set the pattern for future Spanish–Indian relations. Following the killing

TRIBES OF THE SOUTHWEST CULTURE AREA

Akimel O'odham	Navajo
(*Pima*)	Opata
Apache	Pima Bajo
Cocopa	Pueblo
Cora	Quechan
Guarijio	Seri
Havasupai	Tarahumara
Hopi	Tepehuan
Hualapai	Tohono O'odham
Huichol	(*Papago*)
Karankawa	Tubar
Maricopa	Yaqui
Mayo	Yavapai
Mojave	Zuni

of a Spanish detachment by Pueblo warriors, de Onate launched a major military expedition against the town of Acoma, and on 24 January 1599 his troops massacred some 800 Pueblo citizens and drove another 600 into slavery. For good measure, all male prisoners had one foot amputated.

Yet the Spaniards faced more substantial resistance when they encountered the Apaches. The Apaches resented not only the threat to their territories, but also the destruction of Pueblo communities, with whom they traded. Note that the Apaches did not face the Spanish as a homogenous and united body. In fact, even the individual Apache groupings were themselves separated up into various families, bands and clans, these coming together in temporary cooperation from time to time when facing a mutual threat. By the seventeenth century, this mutual threat was clearly identified as the Spanish, and from c.1630 the Apaches began a formidable campaign of raiding against Spanish settlements. Contemporary Spanish sources relate how the populations of some settlements were under virtual curfew, unable to venture out after early evening because of the threat of swift death at the hands of lurking Apache bands. Conrad Malte-Brun, an early nineteenth-century ethnographer, wrote a book entitled *Universal Geography* (published in 1829), which in its entry on the Apache peoples provides some additional context to the Indian war with the Spaniards:

'These implacable enemies of the Spaniards infest the whole eastern boundary of this country, from the black mountains to the confines of Cohahuila, keeping the inhabitants of several provinces in an incessant state of alarm. There has never been any thing but short skirmishes with them, and although their number has been considerably diminished by wars and frequent famine, the Spaniards are obliged constantly to keep up an establishment of 2000 dragoons, for the purpose of escorting their caravans, protecting their villages, and repelling these attacks, which are perpetually renewed. At first the Spaniards endeavoured to reduce to slavery those who, by the fate of war, fell into their hands; but seeing them indefatigably surmount every obstacle that opposed their return to their dear native mountains,

APACHE WARRIOR
The Mescalero Apache warrior here is armed with an exceptionally long lance, decorated with fur sections and feathers, plus a medicine shield for protection. In terms of clothing, he wears a fur turban plus a painted buckskin shirt and buckskin leggings. Southwestern shields were typically made from thick layers of buckskin, and some varieties were even designed to fold down when not in use.

their conquerors adopted the expedient of sending their prisoners to the island of Cuba, where, from the change of climate, they speedily perished. No sooner were the Apaches informed of this circumstance than they refused any longer either to give or receive quarter. From that moment none have ever been taken prisoners, except those who are surprised asleep, or disabled during the combat.'

> *— Malte-Brun (1829)*

PUEBLO SETTLEMENTS 1700

The Pueblo Indians were, by the beginning of the eighteenth century, spread throughout modern New Mexico and Arizona. Each Pueblo settlement was a distinct social entity, with its own internal system of governance. Yet all the settlements retained cultural and sometimes military alliances.

Malte-Brun presents a fairly accurate portrayal of the early Spanish–Indian conflict, with the Spaniards having to commit major resources in the New Mexican territories just to ensure the operation of daily life. Furthermore, the passage ends with a reflection on the brutal nature of the conflict, which eventually led Spaniards, Mexicans and Americans alike to place bounties on Apache scalps collected, including those of women and children.

The Spanish policy of Apache extermination did not play out as intended. Aided by the Pueblo Revolt of 1680, the Apaches managed to eject the Spanish from New Mexico, although the settlers clawed back their territories over the next 12 years and improved security by establishing *presidios* (fortified bases) along their frontier territories. The Apache raids nevertheless continued unabated throughout most of the eighteenth century, until more subtle Spanish

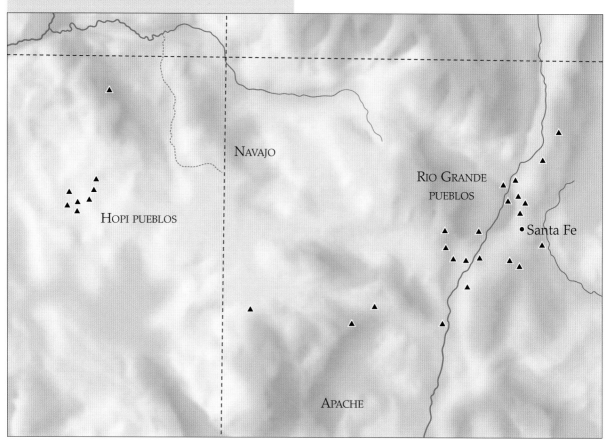

tactics in the 1780s brought greater results. By fostering conflict *between* the Apache tribes, through giving some less belligerent groups preferential Spanish protection, and plying these peoples with alcohol, the Spanish regained a measure of control during the late eighteenth and early nineteenth century. Thousands of Apaches entered new, grim lives on the reservations.

The Effects of Alcohol

The introduction of alcohol by the settlers into Native American society across North America had a significant effect on the ability of the Indians to resist their enemies. Many Native American peoples have a

APACHE TERRITORY 1800

This map of Apache territory at the beginning of the nineteenth century clearly shows how the Apaches separated out into distinct tribal pockets. Apache groups were found in Arizona, New Mexico, Texas, Mexico, Colorado and Oklahoma.

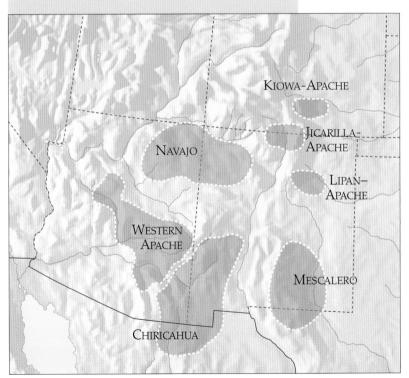

▲ **The Pueblo Revolt, 1680. Spanish soldiers turn their swords and firearms on the Pueblo Indians. It took the Spanish 12 years to bring the rebellion fully under control.**

near-allergic reaction to grain alcohol, and the ability to induce stupefaction was quickly appreciated by the settlers during the seventeenth century, when they were more than happy to turn Indians into alcoholics.

The effects of alcohol are clearly described by the Apache warrior Geronimo, whom we shall encounter later in this chapter. During the 1860s, in one of his operations against the Mexicans, he encountered a mule train with a very special cargo. Here he describes (he provided an autobiography in the early twentieth century) what happened next:

'We attacked several settlements in the neighborhood and secured plenty of provisions and supplies. After about three days we attacked and captured a mule pack train at a place called by the Indians "Pontoco". It is situated in the mountains due west, about one day's journey from Arispe.

There were three drivers with this train. One was killed and two escaped. The train was loaded with mescal, which was contained in bottles held in wicker baskets. As soon as we made camp the Indians began to get drunk and fight each other. I, too, drank enough mescal to feel the effect of it, but I was not drunk. I ordered the fighting stopped, but the order was disobeyed. Soon almost a general fight was in progress. I tried to place a guard out around the camp, but all were drunk and refused to serve. I expected an attack from Mexican troops at any moment, and really it was a serious matter to me, for being in command I would be held responsible for any ill luck attending the expedition. Finally the camp became comparatively still, for the Indians were too drunk to walk or even fight. While they were in this stupor I poured out all the mescal, then I put out all the fires and moved the pack mules to a considerable distance from the camp.'

— *Barrett* (1906)

The disorder brought about by alcohol, as witnessed in this incident, reached epidemic proportions amongst many Native American tribes, and bred dependence upon European suppliers to feed the subsequent addictions. Alcoholism remains a significant problem amongst Native American peoples even today, with much higher percentage rates of alcohol abuse than many other sectors of American society, a sad legacy of the clash of cultures.

New Enemies

In 1821, Mexico declared its independence from Spain. It was the catalyst for a new wave of hostility between the Apaches and the settlers. Problems arose as the cash-strapped Mexican government let the *presidio* system slide; it also had less cash available to maintain basic living conditions on the Indian reservations. During the 1820s, therefore, Apache raiding became more vigorous, with a particularly insidious response from the Mexicans, as the historian Jason Hook explains in the quotation, left.

A cruel state of warfare existed between the Indians and the Mexicans for the next decade, at which point came a major political change for the region and for the Apaches. The Treaty of Guadalupe Hidalgo, signed in 1848, transferred the southwestern territories to the United States, and established permanent borders between the United States and Mexico. While the treaty was principally focused on territorial divisions and rights of citizenship, its Article XI acknowledged the issue of Indian raiding into Mexican territory:

'Considering that a great part of the territories, which, by the present treaty, are to be comprehended for the future within the limits of the United States, is now occupied by savage tribes, who will hereafter be under the exclusive control of the Government of the United States, and whose incursions within the territory of Mexico would be prejudicial in the extreme, it is solemnly agreed that all such incursions shall be forcibly restrained by the Government of the United States whensoever this may be necessary; and that when they cannot be prevented, they shall be

'THE DEEPLY-INGRAINED APACHE HATRED OF THE MEXICANS WAS INTENSIFIED WHEN, IN 1825, THE GOVERNOR OF SONORA OFFERED A BOUNTY OF 100 PESOS ($100) FOR THE SCALP OF ANY APACHE WARRIOR OVER FOURTEEN. THIS BOUNTY WAS IMITATED BY CHIHUAHUA PROVINCE IN 1837, AND WAS EVEN EXTENDED TO 50 PESOS FOR WOMEN'S SCALPS AND 25 PESOS FOR THOSE OF CHILDREN.'

— HOOK (1987)

MANGAS COLORADOS AND THE COPPERMINE MIMBREÑOS

The Coppermine Mimbreños was the name applied to those Apaches who worked in the Mexican copper mines at Santa Rita. Headed by their leader, Juan José Compá, the Indians had apparently stable relations with the local Mexicans. All this changed in 1837, when they, along with Compá, were invited to a feast organized by the American trader James Johnson. Unknown to the Indians as they ate and drank, their feast table was the target of a Mexican howitzer, hidden and loaded with grapeshot. Johnson gave the order for the gun to fire, and the artillery piece and small-arms fire slaughtered the dinner party to a man. The scalps of those killed were then traded for a bounty. Indian retaliation came in the form of Mangas Colorados, an eastern Apache leader known for his physical stature and aggressive warrior spirit. Related to Compá, Colorados vented his fury on the local Mexicans and Americans, killing 22 American miners in one incident alone.

After he was caught and beaten by a similar group of miners in April 1851, Colorados became increasingly violent, ordering the killing of anyone seen wearing a hat (Apaches customarily did not wear hats, so their targets were easily identified).

▲ **A fairly accurate representation of Apache warriors on the move. The lead figure appears in much the same attire as Mangas Colorados, including the red bandana and settler-style jacket.**

punished by the said Government, and satisfaction for the same shall be exacted in the same way, and with equal diligence and energy, as if the same incursions were meditated or committed within its own territory, against its own citizens.'

The treaty was strong in spirit, but initially weak in body. Apache warriors continued to raid across the Mexican border, and US attempts to control this activity were limited. Yet the Apaches were soon having problems with American settlers, particularly from the miners who sought to exploit traditional Apache lands. The Mimbreños warrior chief, Mangas Colorados, (see feature box, above) launched a virtual war on the American settlers, a war in which he found a new ally in the tribal leader of the Central Chiricahua, Cochise. They began what became known as the Apache Wars, which ran in an uneven fashion from 1861 to 1886 and cost hundreds of settler and Native American lives.

The Battle of Apache Pass

For the first four years of the Apache Wars, the Native Americans were aided by a major US distraction in the form of the American Civil War. The first Apache–American battle, however, came in 1862,

▶ **Cochise (1823–74) was one of the greatest of the Apache warrior chiefs. During the 1860s and 1870s, he led his warriors against the Arizona settlers, often disappearing into Mexico to escape pursuers.**

when General James Henry Carleton and his California Volunteers campaigned against the Confederates in New Mexico and Arizona. On 14 July, a column of 140 Union troops of the 1st California Cavalry entered the Apache Pass in southern Arizona, confident that they could move through to pass unhindered by the local Apache warriors – negotiations three weeks earlier saw the Apaches give assurances that they could pass through their territory. Once the troops had entered Apache Pass, however, a large Apache force, headed by Colorados and Cochise and aided by future warrior luminaries such as Victorio and Geronimo, attacked, sniping at them from elevated positions. Despite being dehydrated and exhausted, the American troops fought back with dash, elevating

AMERICAN EXPANSION 1818–53

The first half of the nineteenth century saw major changes in both the patterns of settler expansion and the political ownership of the country. By the 1850s, the southwest was essentially under US control, the Americans having acquired territory from the Mexicans through war and treaty.

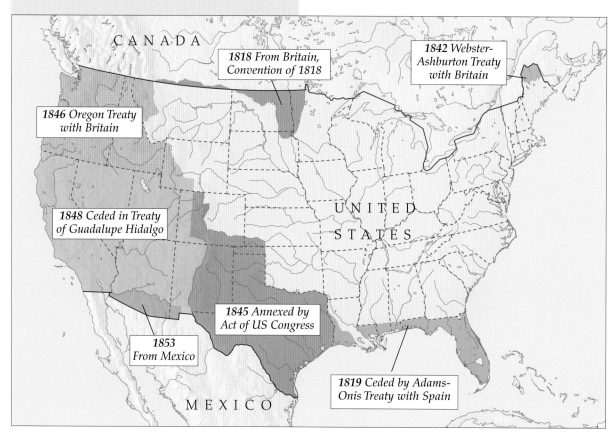

CANADA

1818 From Britain, Convention of 1818

1842 Webster-Ashburton Treaty with Britain

1846 Oregon Treaty with Britain

1848 Ceded in Treaty of Guadalupe Hidalgo

UNITED STATES

1845 Annexed by Act of US Congress

1853 From Mexico

1819 Ceded by Adams-Onis Treaty with Spain

MEXICO

Apache brands into an anti-US coalition, while the US invested in strengthening its defences in the region, including the building of Fort Bowie to guard Apache Pass.

Following the Battle of Apache Pass, Carleton's campaigns against the Indians sharpened, and the levels of brutality increased. Colorados was captured and tortured to death in 1863, and Carleton employed the ruthlessly effective Colonel Christopher 'Kit' Carson in a war to subdue the Navajo and Mescalero, forcing thousands of them into the Bosque Rendondo Reservation (essentially a brutal prison camp). Carson waged a localized version of total war on the Native Americans, attacking their sources of food and tribal supply lines. His campaign resulted in the 'Long Walk' of the Navajo, a forced exodus of 482km (300 miles) undertaken by 9000 people, mostly travelling on foot. Hundreds died of exhaustion or execution on the journey, and many more died in the appalling conditions at the Bosque Redondo. The Long Walk was one of the most shameful episodes of

▲ The Apache Indian chief Victorio (1825–80), here photographed in 1877, was an experienced warrior by the time he reached 20 years old and, after a life of war, died in battle in 1880.

the Apache Wars, and cast a lasting shadow over Carson's reputation.

Crook's Campaigns

The US Government and Army constructed a number of camps and reservations throughout the southwest, designed to contain and assimilate compliant Native Americans. Being in a reservation, however, did not

their howitzers and blasting the positions above them. The fight petered out inconclusively, with about 10 Apache dead compared to two Union fatalities, but it had the effect of drawing the various

THE MOHAVE INDIANS

Away from the Apache territories, inhabiting the Arizona-California border, the Mohave Indians also underwent a traumatic social transformation during the mid- to late nineteenth century. During the 1850s, the Mohave were at war both with rival Native American tribes – particularly the Maricopa, Pima and Papago – and the US settlers who moved into Mohave territory in search of gold, the former conflict weakening the Mohave's capabilities to fight the latter. Mohave attacks on settlers resulted in the US Government establishing protective forts and deploying significant numbers of troops. A major clash between the Mohave warriors and soldiers of the US 6th Infantry brought a signal defeat for the Indians, and their power gradually attenuated during the rest of the century as they were progressively forced onto reservations.

▲ A group of Mohave Indians posed for the camera, armed with a mixture of carbines, rifles and handguns. The Mohave clashed in some bitter battles with settler gold prospectors.

▲ Resettled Navajos use adobe bricks to construct living quarters for Union soldiers while under armed guard. The location is the remote Bosque Redondo, a place notorious for its inhumane conditions for Indian captives.

necessarily ensure protection from settler violence. On the morning of 30 April 1871, a large gang of local American vigilantes descended on the Apache inhabitants of Camp Grant, an ill-guarded US military base. Although the camp was, at the time of the attack, inhabited mainly by old people, women and children, this did not stop the vigilantes clubbing or shooting to death 117 people, based on their belief that the Camp Grant Indians were responsible for attacks on settlers around southern Arizona.

The US Government responded by establishing its 'peace policy', which basically involved forced resettlement of Apache tribes on more reservations. The Navajos and various other Indian tribes signed peace treaties with the Federal Government, although the terms of mutual respect accorded by the legalistic language of the treaties fell far short in reality. Led by General George Crook, the commander of the Department of Arizona, US forces in the region conducted pitiless campaigns against those Apaches who proved stubbornly resistant. Crook had a talent for turning the Apaches against one another, employing large numbers of allied Apache scouts to help track down the enemy war parties hiding in the wilderness. The use of such scouts effectively removed the invisibility that was so important to the Apache style of warfare.

US Army Indian Scouts

It is worthwhile at this point making a deeper study of the US Army Indian Scouts. Scouts were not just recruited from the southwest, but the Apaches, Mohave

ARTICLE I OF THE TREATY BETWEEN THE UNITED STATES OF AMERICA AND THE NAVAJO TRIBE OF INDIANS, CONCLUDED 1 JUNE 1868

From this day forward all war between the parties to this agreement shall for ever cease. The government of the United States desires peace, and its honor is hereby pledged to keep it. The Indians desire peace, and they now pledge their honor to keep it.

If bad men among the whites, or among other people subject to the authority of the United States, shall commit any wrong upon the person or property of the Indians, the United States will, upon proof made to the agent and forwarded to the Commissioner of Indian Affairs at Washington city, proceed at once to cause the offender to be arrested and punished according to the laws of the United States, and also to reimburse the injured persons for the loss sustained.

If bad men among the Indians shall commit a wrong or depredation upon the person or property of any one, white, black, or Indian, subject to the authority of the United States and at peace therewith, the Navajo tribe agree that they will, on proof made to their agent, and on notice by him, deliver up the wrongdoer to the United States, to be tried and punished according to its laws; and in case they wilfully refuse so to do, the person injured shall be reimbursed for his loss from the annuities or other moneys due or to become due them under this treaty, or any others that may be made with the United States. And the President may prescribe such rules and regulations for ascertaining damages under this article as in his judgment may be proper; but no such damage shall be adjusted and paid until examined and passed upon by the Commissioner of Indian Affairs, and no one sustaining loss whilst violating, or because of his violating, the provisions of this treaty or the laws of the United States shall be reimbursed therefore.

▲ Samuel F. Tappan, a signatory on the 1868 Navajo Treaty. Tappan was actually an activist for Native American rights, arguing that civil, not military, law should prevail on the reservations.

▲ Manuelito was one of several Navajo chiefs who put their names to the 1868 treaty. By the time he signed the treaty, he had been fighting the American settlers for more than a decade.

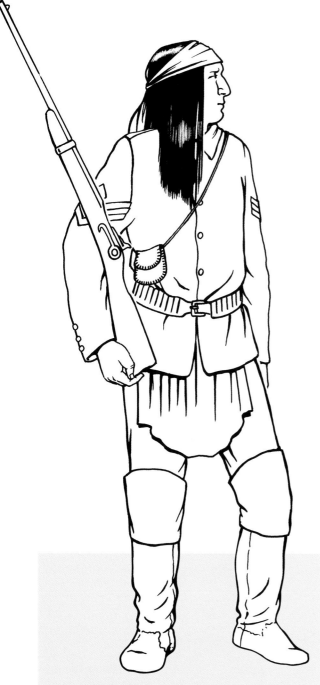

US ARMY APACHE SCOUT
This US Army Apache Scout wears sergeant's stripes, the highest rank typically achieved by Native Americans in US Army employ. He would, however, have little authority over white troops.

and Navajo were all fertile recruiting grounds. Other Native American tribes that provided significant numbers of scouts included the Pawnee, Crow, Osage, Arikara, Seminole and Delaware. The authorization to recruit Indian scouts came with a Congressional Act of 28 July 1866, which stated that:

'The President is authorized to enlist and employ in the Territories and Indian country a force of Indians not to exceed one thousand to act as scouts, who shall receive the pay and allowances of cavalry soldiers, and be discharged whenever the necessity for further employment is abated, at the discretion of the department commander.'

Indian Scouts enlisted for a specified period, typically five years, although on discharge they could re-enlist after a period of three to six months. The US Army Indian Scouts should not be confused with civilian Indian military contractors, who were also called scouts. A civilian scout was a temporary employee of the military forces, and had no rights to obtain rank or to receive a military pension. The military scouts, by contrast, could receive a pension and could also ascend a limited way up the NCO rank ladder.

Indian Scouts' Uniform

The uniform of Indian Scouts varied widely depending on the time and place of their service. Generally speaking, the evolution from 1866 to 1895, when the Indian Scouts were finally merged into the US Army, was from civilian dress embellished with the odd military item through to a formal uniform based on that of the US Army. A scout of 1890, for example, might be seen in a five-button fatigue jacket plus matching trousers, all Army issue, and in that year Apache scouts and others were issued with the US Army Dress Helmet, with an appearance similar to that of a British policeman.

The Indian Scouts, as we have seen, were an integral part of the American military campaign to subdue warring Native Americans. Although their position in Native American history is morally ambiguous, they did lay the groundwork for thousands of Native Americans who went on to serve in the US Armed Forces during the twentieth century.

Geronimo

During the 1870s, the policy of resettlement had brought nothing but hardship and acrimony for the Native Americans, which in turn sowed the seeds for further revolt and conflict. Apache leaders such as Victorio, Juh and Geronimo fled from the massive San Carlos reservation, taking with them large groups of followers and waging an insurgency campaign against Crook's men. Geronimo in particular headed the last great resistance of the Apache Wars. More correctly known by the Indian name of Goyathlay ('One Who

▲ **This group of Indian Scouts presents a mixed bag of clothing and weapons. Although the man on the left has a breechloading carbine, the others are equipped with old muzzle-loading percussion cap rifles.**

Yawns'), Geronimo cut his teeth as a warrior acting as a guide for raids against the Mexicans. He first fled the San Carlos reservation in September 1881, then returned in April 1882 as a raider, killing the chief of police there and fleeing back into the wilderness, taking more warriors with him. Over the next four years, Geronimo was repeatedly captured by, or surrendered

▲ A striking portrait of the great Geronimo. Geronimo fought US and Mexican settlers for several decades, and his talents as a warrior are remembered in the motto of the US Army 501st Infantry Regiment – 'Geronimo'.

to, US troops, only to escape reservation life and return to resistance. In his autobiography, dictated to S. M. Barrett in the early twentieth century, he acknowledged that the US forces had become particularly good at countering his evasive style of warfare:

'Contrary to our expectations the United States soldiers had not left the mountains in Mexico, and were soon trailing us and skirmishing with us almost every day. Four or five times they surprised our camp. One time they surprised us about nine o'clock in the morning, and captured all our horses (nineteen in number) and secured our store of dried meats. We also lost three Indians in this encounter. About the middle of the afternoon of the same day we attacked them from the rear as they were passing through a prairie – killed one soldier, but lost none ourselves. In this skirmish we recovered all our horses except three that belonged to me. The three horses that we did not recover were the best riding horses we had.'

— Barrett (1906)

Geronimo's flight finally came to an end in September 1886, when he surrendered for the last time. His surrender brought to a close half a century of war between the Apaches and the Americans. The Apaches had been finally quieted, but only at the cost of much American, Mexican and Spanish blood.

APACHE TACTICS

By now we have become somewhat familiar with the impressive physical powers of the Native Americans. The Indians of the southwest, however, took endurance and affinity with the wilderness to near-supernatural levels. From the earliest age, Southwest Indian children, male and female, were acclimatized to the realities of their natural surroundings. For the

▼ **Under military supervision at the desolate San Carlos Reservation, Apaches dig an irrigation ditch as part of plan to turn what was a nomadic tribe into sedentary farmers. Such forced lifestyles generated much resistance from the Apache people.**

GERONIMO

▲ **White Mountain Apache are mustered at a Southern Pacific Railway Station by a US Army officer for the pursuit of the hostile Apache chief Geronimo. Such scouts were essential for catching the wily outlaw.**

the endurance so characteristic of the Apaches. Boys were hardened by rough wrestling games and mock battles, and taught by their relatives the geography, attributes and sanctity of their surroundings.'

– Hook (1987)

Tactical Withdrawals

Such conditioning created young male warriors with a impressive and wide-ranging understanding of the landscape and exceptional powers of endurance. The latter were an integral part of Southwest Indian warfare, as they gave a whole new meaning to the military term 'tactical withdrawal'. A common ploy of the Southwest Indians was to engage the enemy in a brief, furious ambush and then melt like ghosts back into the landscape. Spanish, Mexican or American troops would often then

boys, this process of hardening not only served the purposes of hunting, but also those of warfare:

'The Apaches were trained for war from boyhood. Boys woke early and bathed in the river, even if they had to crack the surface ice to do so. They ran up hillsides and back with a mouthful of water, to learn correct breathing through the nose, and

set off in pursuit of their enemy, but were actually falling into a trap. The Indian warriors, who could comfortably cover tens of kilometres on foot every day, even under the blistering desert sun, would keep the enemy pursuit alive through providing tantalizing glimpses and signs.

Meanwhile, the less-hardened settlers would begin to suffer from exhaustion and dehydration, leaving them exposed to a sudden counter-attack when they were least able to resist it. Once the settlers were in retreat, however, the Indians were just

▲ **An Apache raiding party heads out. Such parties were generally kept small – less than a dozen people – as it was easier to gain the advantage of surprise with fewer numbers in tow.**

as inexhaustible in their pursuit, harrying their enemy constantly and killing or capturing any individuals who strayed far from the group.

The Southwest Indians soon understood that the settlers were not at home in the wilderness they attempt to colonize, and turned this to their advantage. For example, during feigned retreats the Indians would deliberately create zigzagging and convoluted routes for the pursuers, taking them away from frequently travelled, familiar trails and into countryside in which large amounts of equipment became an encumbrance, commanders became disorientated and wagons became stuck or damaged.

The exhaustion and confusion of hunting the Southwest Indians is nowhere more eloquently described than in John G. Bourke's *On the Border with Crook,* published in 1891. Bourke's accounts of fighting the Apache reveals something of why the Apache Wars dragged on for such a long time:

'No serpent can surpass him in cunning; he will dodge and twist and bend in all directions, boxing the compass, doubling like a fox, scattering his party the moment a piece of rocky ground is reached over which it would, under the best circumstances, be difficult to follow. Instead of moving in file, his party will here break into a skirmishing order, covering a broad space and diverging at the most unexpected moment from the primitive direction, and not perhaps reuniting for miles. Pursuit is retarded and very frequently baffled … In the meantime the Apache raiders, who know full well that the pursuit must slacken for a while, have reunited at some designated hill, or near some spring or "water tank", and are pushing across the high mountains as fast as legs harder than leather can carry them … At the summit of each ridge, concealed behind rocks or

▲ **Apaches brandish their weapons as they charge into an attack. The rocky terrain of the arid southwest provided perfect opportunities for channelling enemies into narrow passes and defiles.**

trees, a few picked men, generally not more than two or three, will remain waiting for the approach of the pursuit.'

– *Bourke (1891)*

From this description, it becomes apparent why the settlers had to turn to Indian Scouts to pursue the Apaches and other Southwest Indians. As General Crook once commented: 'To polish a diamond, there is nothing like its own dust.' Bourke goes on to explain the purpose of the small rearguard groups of Apache, noting that as the pursuers approached they would open fire with firearms or bows for a few seconds, causing the soldiers to halt, bunch up and go to ground. While the soldiers waited to see how the attack would play out, the Apache were back on

their feet or horses, and moving quickly away from the scene. By playing this tactic out repeatedly, the settlers' units were compelled to move in fits and starts, exhausting themselves in the process. Probing attacks delivered at night also ensured that the settlers did not get any rest when the sun fell.

Ambush

As with so many Indian tactics, the tactical withdrawal was often the build-up to a deliberate ambush. Much of the territory of the southwest was eminently suitable for ambush tactics, with high, rocky terrain split by narrow passes that formed natural choke points for anybody travelling through the territory. Simultaneous fire was the key to an effective ambush, made more so by the prodigious talents of the Southwest Indians with bows and firearms. The typical ambush involved a group of one or two dozen warriors, positioned strategically along a pass or trail. Much like modern anti-tank tactics,

COMMUNICATIONS

In his account of the battle against the Apache, John G. Bourke also relates how the Apache communicated with one another during their operations. They relied heavily on ground signals to coordinate their actions against a common enemy, typical signals being the following:

- An inscription or pictograph drawn on the bark of a sycamore tree.

- An inscription or pictograph drawn on a smooth-faced rock, often beneath an overhanging ledge to protect the image from the elements.

- A knot tied in a flexible branch or clump of grasses.

- One or several stones placed against the trunk of a tree.

- A sapling leaned up against another tree.

- A piece of buckskin laid over a branch.

company must pass through a mountain defile. We reserved fire until all of the troops had passed through; then the signal was given. The Mexican troopers, seemingly without a word of command, dismounted, and placing their horses on the outside of the company, for breastworks, made a good fight against us. I saw that we could not dislodge them without using all our ammunition, so I led a charge.'

– Barrett (1906)

The description of the ambush illustrates how ammunition conservation was always a consideration for the Indians, and anything more than a small party of enemy would probably require some element of hand-to-hand fighting to destroy. His explanation of the Mexican response also indicates that the settlers were gradually becoming accustomed to the ambush tactic, learning the correct response of finding immediate cover from which to deliver heavy return fire. Geronimo goes on to explain the close-quarters clash that followed:

the Indians would wait for the enemy column to enter the 'kill zone', at which point they would unleash coordinated fire, targeting officers and those manning heavy weapons in particular.

The Apache Geronimo has, as we have seen, done historians a great service by leaving his autobiography to posterity. In his account, he usefully describes the process of ambushing a column of Mexican troops in the Sierra de Sahuaripa Mountains during the summer of 1860:

'The second day in these mountains our scouts discovered mounted Mexican troops. There was only one company of cavalry in this command, and I thought that by properly surprising them we could defeat them. We ambushed the trail over which they were to come. This was at a place where the whole

APACHE MOCCASINS

Apache moccasins were not simply warm, durable footwear – their tough rawhide soles provided good adhesion when climbing across rocks, and created near silent footfalls when stalking or escaping from an enemy. The uppers were made from soft buckskin, and decorated with beads and tassels.

▲ Apache ambush – a painting by Frederic Remington. The Apache, like many Native Americans, proved to be excellent marksmen, a lifetime's training with the bow bringing a natural sense of accuracy.

'The warriors suddenly pressed in from all sides and we fought hand to hand. During this encounter I raised my spear to kill a Mexican soldier just as he leveled his gun at me; I was advancing rapidly, and my foot slipping in a pool of blood, I fell under the Mexican trooper. He struck me over the head with the butt of his gun, knocking me senseless. Just at that instant a warrior who followed in my footsteps killed the Mexican with a spear. In a few minutes not a Mexican soldier was left alive. When the Apache war-cry had died away, and their enemies had been scalped, they began to care for their dead and wounded. I was found lying unconscious where I had fallen. They bathed my head in cold water and restored me to consciousness. Then they bound up my wound and the next morning, although weak from loss of blood and suffering from a severe headache, I was able to march on the return to Arizona. I did not fully recover for months, and I still wear the scar given me by that musketeer. In this fight we had lost so heavily that there really was no glory in our victory, and we returned to Arizona. No one seemed to want to go on the war path again that year.'

– Barrett (1906)

The vigour, surprise and violence of the Apache ambush results in the complete destruction of the Mexican force, although Geronimo's experience illustrates that all such attacks carried major risks of their own.

As we have seen above in our analysis of the Apaches, ambush tactics were not always successful – if the settler troops could bring their typically superior firepower to bear, then the battle could be tipped in their favour. Even if the overall outcome of an ambush was positive, heavy return fire from the ambushed soldiers could turn an Indian victory into a pyrrhic one. For example, in late March 1854, soldiers of the US 1st Cavalry Regiment in New Mexico made a patrol out from their camp at Cantonment Burgwin, some 16km (10 miles) southeast of Taos. During the patrol, a unit of 1st Dragoons, 60 men strong, launched an unauthorized attack on a Jicarilla Apache camp near Pilar, inciting the wrath of local Apache and Ute Indians. In response, the Indians prepared an ambush for the American soldiers, gathering some 200 warriors for the purpose.

The Indians took up position in an area of ravine-split terrain, and at around 8.00 a.m. on 30 March, a coordinated war whoop split the morning silence as the Indians unleashed musket and bow fire on the passing American column. Contemporary accounts of the subsequent battle are somewhat contradictory, but we know that the clash lasted between two and four hours and resulted in the US column suffering 22 dead and 36 wounded – a casualty rate approaching 100 per cent. Twenty-two horses were also lost. The ambush was in one sense an emphatic victory for the Indian warriors, but the battle cost them around 50 warriors killed, and an unknown number wounded.

The Battle of Skeleton Cave

The firepower possessed by the settlers during the second half of the nineteenth century meant that even positions offering apparently excellent cover could be vulnerable. For example, in June 1871 General Crook was appointed to suppress the Indians of Arizona, including those of the Yavapai tribe. The Yavapai were a relatively small group of Indians who had historically allied themselves with the Northern Tonto Apache tribe. Hence when Crook set out on his mission of subjugation, the Yavapai also became targets.

▲ Apaches attacking refugees from Santa Rita. Those captured by the Apache faced either immediate execution, imprisonment (typically reserved for women or children), or, less commonly, a slow death by torture back in the Apache village.

▲ Tombstone, Arizona, 1886. This rare photograph shows the Apache leader Geronimo (left), sat in conference with General George Crook on the far right. Geronimo escaped from Crook's custody on two occasions, much to Crook's embarrassment.

On 28 December 1872, Crook's force – which consisted of three companies of the 5th Cavalry under Captain William H. Brown and utilized the skills of 30 Indian Scouts – finally detected a body of some 110 Yavapai hiding in the mouth of the large Skeleton Cave (also known as Skull Cave) high up in Salt River Canyon.

The American troops surrounded the cave, and when the Indians went to leave Brown announced his presence, and ordered the Indians to surrender. They refused, retreating quickly back into the large cave with American bullets whizzing around their ears. Once inside the recesses of the cave, the Yavapai felt confident of their survival, as the Americans could not see their targets properly to shoot with any real accuracy.

Recognizing this fact, however, Brown ordered his troops to fire their weapons at the roof and walls of the cave, this producing hails of ricochets that tore into the ranks of the sheltering Indians. The effect was ghastly – a total of 76 Indians died and 37 were wounded. Those who surrendered began life imprisonment or the move to reservations. In this instance, their

THE APACHE WAY OF WAR

A useful insight into the Apache way of war came from the pen of Miguel Venegas, whose *A natural and civil history of California* of 1759 contains a useful description of not only the Apache treatment of prisoners, but also of their clothing, tactics and martial character:

'According to some prisoners who have been ransomed, they are extremely savage and brutal; they have very little cultivated land, nor does their country supply them with any plenty of spontaneous productions. They are cruel to those who have the misfortune to fall into their hands; and among them are several apostates. They go entirely naked, but make their incursions on horses of great swiftness, which they have stolen from other parts, a skin serving them for a saddle. Of the same skins they make little boots or shoes of one piece; and by these they are traced in their flight. They begin the attack with shouts, at a great distance, to strike the enemy with terror. They have not naturally any great share of courage; but the little they can boast of, is extravagantly increased on any good success. In war they rather depend on artifice than valour; and on any defeat submit to the most ignominious terms, but keep their treaties no longer than suits their conveniency. His majesty has ordered, that if they require peace, it should be granted; and even offered to them before they are attacked. But this generosity they construe to proceed from fear. Their arms are the common bows and arrows of the country. The intention of their incursions is plunder, especially horses, which they use both for riding and eating; the flesh of these creatures being one of their greatest dainties.'

—*Venegas* (1759)

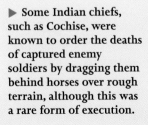 ▶ Some Indian chiefs, such as Cochise, were known to order the deaths of captured enemy soldiers by dragging them behind horses over rough terrain, although this was a rare form of execution.

knowledge of the terrain provided the Indians with no relief from the potent firepower possessed by the Federal Army.

WARFARE AND RAIDING

As historians such as Jason Hook have described, the Apache Indians made a distinction between the practices of 'warfare' and 'raiding'. The purpose of the former was essentially to unleash death upon the enemy, while the latter had the customary objectives of obtaining food, settling scores, and so on, as we have already seen.

Warfare

Open warfare between Southwestern tribes could follow quite formulaic patterns, and frequently involved individual combat among prestigious warriors. In an account of one battle between Yuma and Maricopa Indians in 1842, the Yuma Indians formed themselves into a battle-line headed by two of their chiefs, who walked in front. In contrast to the tactics of evasion and escape described above, here the Yumas approached the Mariocopa village (their objective) quite openly, the two sides forming up in opposing battle lines. When the warriors had gathered, one of the Yuma chiefs stood in front of his Mariocopa counterpart, and offered a challenge. The two men then engaged in single combat, resulting in the death of the Yuma chief, at which point the battle became general, with the respective lines engaging one another. On other occasions, the general clash between opposing sides might actually be resolved by individual or small-group combat, rather than risk the killing of too many warriors in a prolonged battle.

The tribes of the southwest frequently made alliances with one another for purposes of strengthening their warmaking capability. The

◀ Apaches on horseback, photographed in the late nineteenth century. The effect of the settlers on the Apache way of life was profound. Previously, the Apache had enjoyed the freedom of vast tracts of land, across which they hunted and journeyed. The settler expansion caused the collapse of Apache culture.

negotiation are observed. Any band wishing to go to war sends messengers, asking its friends to furnish warriors for an expedition. This mission bears with it the council pipe, and is accompanied by ponies as presents, to encourage the favorable consideration of the proposition. A council is held in which the whole matter is fully discussed. If the band accepts the pipe and smokes, the request is granted, and the warriors of the band, or rather such as choose, extend their co-operation. After this ceremony, warriors from all the bands rendezvous at a given point, and start upon their errand of atrocity and spoliation. To decline acceding to the proposition to take the war-path, frequently occurs from policy or necessity. The band seeking for assistance, if not successful in gathering a sufficient number of warriors to make up the necessary strength, abandons its project.'

– Keim (1825)

process of negotiating these alliances was, as one writer of the early nineteenth century described, an activity laced with etiquette and ritual:

'In the organization of war-parties, composed of warriors of the different tribes, certain ceremonies of

The process of making an allied war party is here seen as a delicate matter of mutual respect, but also of reason – the band approached for the alliance considers its position carefully, and it is obvious that there was not an automatic guarantee that a request

APACHE MEDICINE STRANDS
Indian medicine strands were used to confer spiritual protection or animalistic powers upon the wearer. Feathers, pieces of animal skin, scalps and rattlesnake rattles were common adornments, each element carrying its own symbolism for the tribal members.

▲ Navajo shamans gather in full ceremonial outfits to perform a ritual. The settlers attempted to discourage shamanism, which as the Ghost Dance rebellion of the 1890s proved, could be a focus for Indian resistance.

for an alliance would be granted. War parties of any description were highly ritualistic affairs, preceded by much ceremony. In Apache warmaking, the village shaman would conduct various rites before the party set off, the sage chanting prayers for safety and success. He would also accompany the war party on its outward journey to battle, ensuring that his magic accompanied the fighters all the way to their objective. The warriors also carried small buckskin bags holding a yellow powder known as *hoddentin*, made from the pollen of the cattail, a plant sacred to the Apache. The substance had broad ceremonial

▶ *Hoddentin* powder, sprinkled over the face of this Native American woman, was typically used for ritualistic purposes. It was believed to hold a variety of spiritual powers, from bringing protection to a warrior to the healing of the sick.

applications, ranging from the healing of the sick through to puberty ceremonies for adolescent Apache girls. When setting out on a raid or heading for a battle, each Apache warrior would hold up a small amount of the *hoddentin* to the sun or rub some on his body or tongue.

The shaman watched over any adolescents who were accompanying a war party for the first time. Such boys were blessed by scatterings of *hoddentin* when they left the camp, and the shaman also issued special blessed items of clothing, such as a war cap. The novice warrior was essentially on probation for the first four raids he went on. At first his role was supportive only – he would go and fetch food and water for the other warriors, and act as a guard over the camp at night. If he performed well over the course of the first four raids, he was granted full warrior status, and entered the ranks of the other Apache fighting men.

Raiding

When it came to raiding, the Southwestern Indians conducted their operations in largely the same manner as the other Indian tribes already described in this book. A particularly effective strategy used by the Apaches against the settlers was to raid several locations at once, thereby confusing the required coordinated response. Bourke mentions this strategy, which he saw as particularly acute during the winter of 1870 and the spring of 1871:

'The enemy resorted to a system of tactics which had often been tried in the past and always with success. A number of simultaneous attacks were made at points widely separated, thus confusing both troops and settlers, spreading a vague sense of fear over all the territory infested, and imposing upon the soldiery an exceptional amount of work of the hardest possible kind.'

– Bourke (1891)

Raids in the southwest could range in scale from a dozen warriors stealing a neighbouring tribe's horses up to a major action against a well-defended settler outpost. One of the largest raids ever found on record was that attempted by the Navajo Indians in April 1860 against the US Army outpost of Fort

▲ An Apache raiding party attacks a white settler family's home, burning the house and scalping members of the family. Such images, not always based on fact, inspired a vicious hostility towards the Indians.

Defiance. Fort Defiance had been built in 1851 in what is now Arizona as a defence against Navajo raids on local settlers, although the fort seemed superfluous after a peace agreement was reached in 1858. Reconciliation, however, was matched by an equal amount of mutual suspicion, and the US commander at Santa Fe, New Mexico, Colonel Benjamin Bonneville, made regular aggressive patrols around Fort Defiance, and also held 21 Indian prisoners as hostages against the treaty terms.

In January 1860, Navajo–American relations deteriorated, as the Indians began attacks on US supply trains and small isolated outposts. Then, on 30 April, some 1000 Navajo launched a massive attack on Fort Defiance. Reflecting the type of tactics described by Bourke (above), the assault came in from three directions, and managed to take some of the outlying buildings. Only the resistance of three companies of the 3rd Infantry prevented the Indians overrunning Fort Defiance completely, and after two hours of fighting the American troops managed to launch a counter-attack that eventually put the Indians to flight. The US troops had suffered three casualties during the battle, whereas the Navajo lost 12 killed and wounded. The casualties in the battle of Fort Defiance are remarkably light considering the numbers of warriors involved, but it illustrates how the Southwest Indians, as much as the Indians of any other territory, were reluctant to prosecute a battle of long duration, unlike many of the settler forces. It also illustrates how difficult the Indians found tackling well-arranged defences, which here allowed the US troops to take full advantage of their superior firepower.

WEAPONS

Conrad Malte-Brun painted a usefully broad picture of the weapons of the Apaches in the early 1800s, one which provides a context for analysis of Southwest Indians weaponry generally:

'The arrows of the Apaches are three feet [1m] long, and are made of reed or cane, into which they sink a piece of hard-wood, with a point made of iron, bone, or stone. The shot this weapon with such force, that at the distance of 300 paces they can pierce a man. When the arrow is attempted to be drawn out of the wound, the wood detaches itself, and the point remains in the body. Their second offensive weapon is a lance, fifteen feet [4.6m] long. When they charge the enemy they hold this lance with both hands above their head and, at the same

▼ **Navajo Indians gather at Fort Defiance, Arizona, c.1873. The Navajo Indians actually managed to return to their homelands following the Navajo Treaty of 1868. Combined with good trade relations with the settlers, this return resulted in sustained population growth.**

time, guide their horse by pressing him with their knees. Many of them are armed with firelocks, which, as well as the ammunition, they have taken in battle from the Spaniards, who never sell them any. The archers and fusileers combat on foot; but the lancers are

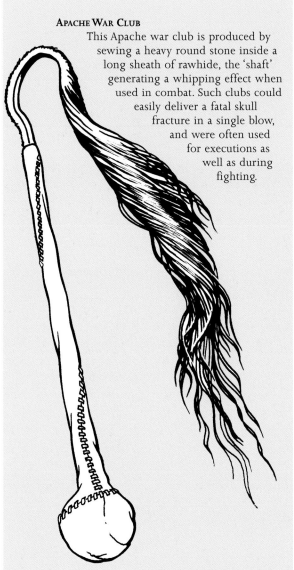

APACHE WAR CLUB
This Apache war club is produced by sewing a heavy round stone inside a long sheath of rawhide, the 'shaft' generating a whipping effect when used in combat. Such clubs could easily deliver a fatal skull fracture in a single blow, and were often used for executions as well as during fighting.

◀ San Juan, a Mescalero Apache chief, stands for his portrait holding a spear and a shield. The line across the shield indicates that it could fold down when not in use, and it is decorated with sun and star motifs. He wears a traditional chief's blanket.

always on horseback. They make use of a buckler for defence. Nothing can equal the impetuosity and address of their horsemen. They are thunderbolts, whose stroke it is impossible to parry or escape.'

— *Malte-Brun* (1829)

Malte-Brun gives a largely accurate account of Apache weaponry and tactics, although with some errors, as we shall see. The traditional weapons of the Southwest Indians were the lance, club, sling and bow,

which they used to great effect even once they had widely adopted 'firelocks' during the eighteenth century. Interestingly, the Southwest Indians also used rudimentary types of swords, at least until their value was lost during the battles against the far better-equipped Spaniards.

One type of sword was entirely wooden and shaped basically like a paddle, the broad edge of the paddle 'sharpened' to form a rudimentary blade. The second principal type of sword had a little more sophistication, and consisted of a shaft around 1m (3ft) long with the edge studded with razor-sharp pieces of obsidian. In determined hands, such a sword was capable of severing a man's head with a single blow, but it still came a poor second to the steel blades of the Spanish *conquistadors*.

The lance is often overlooked in popular representations of the Native American at war, yet it was an integral part of their arsenal. A typical Apache lance would, as Malte-Brun notes, measure up to 4.6m (15ft) long, and was capable of delivering a lethal penetrating wound to anybody caught on the end.

◀ **This postcard of Geronimo is interesting for the close-up of the basic Apache war club. While some war clubs were sewn into hide (see opposite), a more rudimentary but equally effective form of club consisted of a rounded stone bound to the end of a shaft with rawhide thongs.**

▲ **An Apache hunter procuring poison for his arrows by causing a rattlesnake to bite into a deer liver. Arrows heads were then dipped into the liver. Other poison sources included spiders and putrefied meat.**

Bows

Yet where Malte-Brun is in error in his claim that archers would fight only on foot, and not from horseback. Although stalking and raiding tactics meant that this was true in many situations, eyewitness accounts have shown that the Apaches were indeed talented bowmen even from the back of a horse. George Catlin, an American painter, writer and traveller who specialized in the Native Americans as his

subject-matter during the early 1800s, once witnessed a group of Apache warriors performing competitive archery from the back of galloping horses, and was impressed by both their speed and accuracy:

'For this day's sport, which is repeated many times in the year, the ground is chosen on the prairie, level and good for running, and in a semicircle are made ten successive circular targets in the ground by cutting away the turf, and making a sort of 'bull's-eye' in the center, covered with pipe-clay, which is white. Prizes are shot for, and judges are appointed to award them. Each warrior, mounted, in his war costume and war paint, and shoulders naked, and shield upon his back, takes ten arrows in his left hand with his bow, as if going into battle, and galloping their horse around in a circle of a mile or so, under full whip to get them at the highest speed, thus pass in succession the ten targets and give their arrows as they pass. The rapidity with which their arrows are placed upon the string and sent is a mystery to the bystander, and must be seen to be believed. No repeating arms every yet constructed are so rapid, nor any arm, and that little distance, more fatal.'

– Catlin (1868)

The lethality and talent of the Apache archers is obvious, and it is inconceivable that they would not apply such skills in combat, as did tribes such as the Comanche. Malte-Brun's earlier account illustrates how the arrows themselves were designed for maximum physical impact, the sophisticated design including a detachable arrowhead to increase the severity of the wound.

In terms of bow design, the Indians of the southwest used both sinew-backed and self-bows, the latter made from woods such as juniper, yew and ash. James Haley, in his book *Apaches: A History and Cultural Portrait* (1981), has shown how these bows had respectable power and range. He notes that a sinew-backed bow

▲ A young Navajo warrior with bow and arrows. The bow here is a simple piece of wood, probably yew, ash or juniper, but some Southwest Indian tribes' bows were enhanced with strips of sinew to increase their elasticity and therefore improve the release velocity of the arrows.

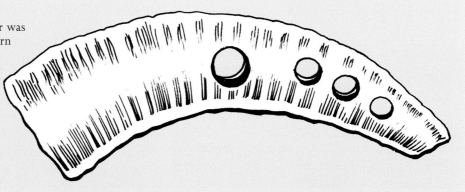

ARROW STRAIGHTENER
The arrow straightener was a piece of wood or horn bored through with perforations. Arrow shafts were passed through the apertures, and the implement used as a wrench to straighten out irregularities in the shaft.

◀ Apaches with percussion cap carbines, late nineteenth century. During this century, Native Americans were keen to get their hands on rifled weapons, which they appreciated for their greater accuracy in hunting and combat.

▶ Fort Wingate, New Mexico. Apache scouts drill with rifles. US Army firearms issued to Native Americans were of variable quality. Many guns were old flintlock muskets crudely rifled and converted to the percussion cap system.

could fire an arrow at 43m (141ft) per second and penetrate Spanish armour. But even the self-bow could accurately fire arrows at 35m (115ft) per second to ranges of more than 100m (328ft). Haley notes that 'arrows striking a tree at short distance frequently drove into the wood until they were not removable – sometimes over halfway; deer shot at short range were usually run through and the arrows recovered beyond' (Haley, 1981).

Firearms

Of course, the Southwest Indians relented to the gradual infiltration of firearms. The Apache and other Southwest Indian tribes lived primarily as hunter-gathers, supplemented by some limited agriculture, and their diet was varied – it included deer, antelope, elk, rabbits, woodrats and, in the eastern territories, buffalo. They also ate horses and mules when necessary. Firearms provided a new and highly

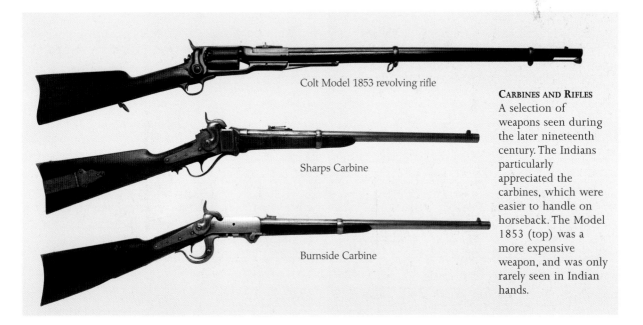

Colt Model 1853 revolving rifle

Sharps Carbine

Burnside Carbine

CARBINES AND RIFLES
A selection of weapons seen during the later nineteenth century. The Indians particularly appreciated the carbines, which were easier to handle on horseback. The Model 1853 (top) was a more expensive weapon, and was only rarely seen in Indian hands.

successful tool for both hunting such diverse prey and for waging war. Furthermore, the prolific employment of Indians as scouts in the US forces meant that many Indians received formal training in the use of firearms, which helped wed them to the practicality of guns. Photographs of Indian warriors from the late nineteenth century reveal an inconsistent distribution of firearms throughout the Southwestern tribes. For example, a photograph of Geronimo and his associates just before his surrender to Crook in 1886 showed the Apaches carrying Springfield and Winchester rifles, various types of handgun as well as the traditional bows and arrows.

SHIELDS AND ARMOUR

Looking back at Malte-Brun's description of Apache warfare, we see his reference to Indian warriors using a 'buckler' – a European term for a small shield. David Jones has observed that 'the southwest fascination with shields equalled that of the Plains warriors and exceeded theirs in producing a greater variety of designs' (Jones, 2004). The constituent elements of the Southwestern shields were typically thick layers of rawhide (horse or bison) or buckskin often stretched over the disk of wood, although in some instances the wood was omitted and the layers of skin simply multiplied to compensate.

A typical Navajo shield, for example, consisted of two thick layers of hide, shaped to measure about 46cm (18in) in diameter when dried. Heavy rawhide stitching was sometimes applied around the rim to strengthen the construction. In some instances, the shield was creased down the middle and capable of being folded away when not in use. The shield was gripped by a small wooden handle. Jones notes that, in the case of the Apaches, 'when fighting on foot with a shield, they were trained to crouch low and extend the shield before them so that they almost disappeared from view as they approached the enemy' (Jones, 2004).

On occasion, particularly during the early inter-tribal battles when no firearms were present, sometimes just a hefty buckskin sufficed to provide a basic shield. In 1928, Leslie Spier wrote an article for the *Anthropological Papers of the American Museum of Natural*

APACHE WARRIOR WITH SHIELD
At Apache warrior crouches down to recce the land before him. He clutches a small round medicine shield; these shields were typically capable of stopping arrows and spears.

MEDICINE SHIELD
The medicine shield above is replete with Apache symbolism. The prevalance of circles is tied to the Apache 'sacred hoop', a symbol of the circle of life from birth to death. Also represented here are teepees and phases of the moon.

History, entitled 'Havasupai Ethnography'. In it he described a raid by Yavapai Indians on a Havasupai camp. During the battle, the Havasupai showed an ingenious use of buckskins as an *ad hoc* form of protection. For stopping arrows, they would drape a large piece of buckskin over a stick or bow, holding it up in front of them as a form of shield. The loose-hanging sheet of hide, even if it didn't entirely stop the passage of an arrow, would certainly alter its course and subtract from its power, providing what modern military engineers would call 'stand-off distance' between the shield and the individual behind it. Furthermore, at one point, the group of Yavapai were trapped and resorted to hurling stones at the Havasupai, which once again were parried by the buckskin shields. Jones notes that 'a number of times, the others were sent back to the Havasupai camp for more deerskins, as the ones in use lost their effectiveness after absorbing rocks and arrows for a number of hours' (Jones, 2004).

In addition to carrying shields, the Southwest Indians also used body armour to protect themselves in battle. Typically this armour was formed by wrapping layers of hide around the torso, such as was typical of the Hopi Indians, or by creating buckskin warshirts, as seen among the various Apache tribes. These warshirts could be particularly hefty, built up from as many as eight layers of thick buckskin, the layers glued together by a powerful adhesive made from cactus leaves. The shirts often had elbow-length sleeves, providing some measure of protection for the arms while in close-quarters combat, but without hampering mobility.

Generally speaking, the heaviest specimens of shirt were worn by mounted warriors (these warshirts often extended to knee length and incorporated splits to allow the warrior to mount and dismount his horse), while the lighter varieties were naturally favoured by those who had to travel and fight on foot.

THE HOPI INDIANS

The Hopi Indians feature little in this chapter, as their physical isolation in tough territories of Arizona, plus their frequent willingness to engage with settler culture, meant that they were largely preserved from the murderous battles of the nineteenth century. During the sixteenth century, however, they came into conflict with the expanding Spanish, particularly against the depredations of the explorer Francisco de Coronado, who in 1541 led a campaign of conquest into Hopi territory. The Hopi put up a patchy resistance to Spanish encroachment, but attempts to convert them to Christianity intensified the fightback, and the Hopi joined in the Pueblo Rebellion of 1680. When this eventually failed, the Hopi relocated many of their settlements to more inaccessible parts of the country, where they continued their attempt to practise their traditional way of life in the face of settler expansion.

◄ A group of Hopi Indians are seen here on a hunting trip, simply armed with spears and rabbit sticks. The rabbit stick was a curved piece of heavy wood, designed to bring down not only rabbits but also other small game and even coyotes. It was thrown at the target animal in a low skimming action, parallel to the ground, and would deliver a stunning blow if it struck.

Hopi rabbit stick

Geronimo's 'Mightiest Battle'

The autobiography of Geronimo has proved invaluable for illuminating our understanding of Southwest Indian warrior culture. A fitting way to end this chapter is to examine what Geronimo termed his 'Mightiest Battle', which occurred during the mid-1880s in Mexico, when Geronimo was once more on the run with his band of followers. His account of this battle pulls together some of threads of this chapter, and provides a good overall picture of how the Southwest Indians coped with a variety of tactical challenges.

The story opens with Geronimo and his followers 'camped in the mountains north of Arispe' (all the quotations given here are from the previously cited Barrett autobiography):

'One night we made camp some distance from the mountains by a stream. There was not much water in the stream, but a deep channel was worn through the prairie, and small trees were beginning to grow here and there along the bank of this stream.

In those days we never camped without placing scouts, for we knew that we were liable to be attacked at any time. The next morning just at daybreak our scouts came in, aroused the camp, and notified us that Mexican troops were approaching. Within five minutes the Mexicans began firing on us. We took to the ditches made by the stream, and had the women and children busy digging these deeper. I gave strict orders to waste no ammunition and keep under cover. We killed many Mexicans that day and in turn lost heavily, for the fight lasted all day. Frequently troops would charge at one point, be repulsed then rally and charge at another point.'

Geronimo's use of security and firepower reads as if written in a military instruction manual. It is apparent that scouts not only acted in tracking and reconnaissance roles during missions, but also as sentries around the perimeter of a camp. Responding to the Mexican fire, Geronimo also gets his people to occupy proper positions of cover, and the auxiliary role of the women and children is particularly interesting, showing how an entire community could contribute to the battle. He also respects the issue of ammunition conservation, already noted earlier in this chapter, and it is likely that simply remaining under cover resulted in diminishing Mexican fire, as they became conscious of their own ammunition depletion. About midday, the Mexicans obviously began to review their options:

'About noon we began to hear them speaking my name with curses. In the afternoon the general came on the field and the fighting became more furious. I gave orders to my warriors to try to kill all the Mexican officers. About three o'clock the general called all the

▲ A captive white boy in an Apache camp.

▲ Geronimo and his braves in battle order.

officers together at the right side of the field. The place where they assembled was not very far from the main stream and a little ditch ran out close to where the officers stood. Cautiously I crawled out of this ditch very close to where the council was being held. The general was an old warrior. The wind was blowing in my direction, so that l could hear all he said, and I understood most of it. This is about what he told them: "Officers, yonder in those ditches is the red devil Geronimo and his hated band. This must be his last day. Ride on him from both sides of the ditches; kill men, women, and children; take no prisoners; dead Indians are what we want. Do not spare your own men; exterminate this band at any cost; I will post the wounded and shoot all deserters; go back to your companies and advance."'

'Kill the Mexican Officers'

Allowing for some licence on the part of the translator, or Geronimo's memory, the Mexicans apparently realized that exchanging fire at a distance from positions of cover was no way to settle the battle with Geronimo. From the Indian point of view, note how Geronimo gives instructions to his warriors to 'kill all the Mexican officers'. His understanding of Mexican command-and-control, highly centralized upon the officers, is apparent, no doubt aided by his ability to understand the Spanish language. At this point, Geronimo took matters into his own hands as he decapitated the Spanish force and began the battle:

'Just as the command to go forward was given I took deliberate aim at the general and he fell. In an instant the ground around me was riddled with bullets; but I was untouched. The Apaches had seen. From all along the ditches arose the fierce war-cry of my people. The columns wavered an instant and then swept on; they did not retreat until our fire had destroyed the front ranks.

After this their fighting was not so fierce, yet they continued to rally and readvance until dark. They also continued to speak my name with threats and curses. That night before the firing had ceased a dozen Indians had crawled out of the ditches and set fire to the long prairie grass behind the Mexican troops. During the confusion that followed we escaped to the mountains.'

Geronimo's killing of the Mexican general seems to establish a tactical and morale advantage in the coming battle, but it still takes disciplined Indian firepower to cut down the Mexican attack. Yet ultimately, Geronimo does not take the fighting to the ultimate conclusion of destroying the enemy force. Instead, sensing that enough work has been done, he creates a fire as a diversion and makes his escape.

This battle is an extraordinary picture of Indian coordination, intelligence and martial spirit. As with so many other Indian battles, the critical command decisions revolve as much around knowing when to withdraw and when to fight, which explains how the Southwest Indians were able to hold out against overwhelming forces for so long.

▲ Geronimo and Natchez.

▲ Geronimo, his son and two picked braves.

CHAPTER 5

West Coast and Plateau/Basin Tribes

'These Savages may, without injustice, be classed lower in the human scale than even the Esquimaux. Equally inanimate and filthy in habit, they do not possess that ingenuity and perseverance which their Northern neighbours can boast. Sullen and lazy, they only rouse themselves when pressed by want.'
— Turner (1836)

This judgement on the Indians of California, from the nineteenth-century lawyer George Turner, is not given here because of any belief in its accuracy. Its value for the historian, however, is a snapshot of the chilling mindset of the American settlers who, as we shall see, effectively implemented an extermination policy against the Native Americans of the west. The language used is almost indistinguishable from that applied by the Nazis to the Jews. Perhaps more than anywhere else, the clash of cultures between the Native Americans and the settlers was at its most extreme in the far west, which in turn had an impact on the manner of warfare practised by the Indians of those territories.

◀ Wary Indians watch the meeting of American explorer John Fremont and courier Archibald Gillespie, who delivers Presidential orders telling Fremont to aid the American invasion of California, at this point (1846) still a part of Mexico.

▲ Early West Coast Indians practice their skills with bow and arrow. Although the range of the bow varied according to its construction, the warrior would be fairly confident of hitting a human-sized target at ranges of 30–50m (98–164ft).

This final chapter takes in several Native American culture areas that together map out almost the whole of the western United States and a strip of western Canada. We are dealing with two (or perhaps three, depending on your perspective) distinct areas of Native American territory.

First, there is the westernmost strip of the United States, bordered by the Pacific Ocean and running from California up to Alaska. Bulging out from this strip towards the lands of the Plains Indians are the Plateau/Great Basin culture areas, the former belonging to the river-laced territories around the Columbia and Fraser Rivers, while the Great Basin refers to the arid and, in parts, mountainous land between the Rocky Mountains and the Sierra Nevada. More than 40 Native American tribes occupied these lands. The breadth of the peoples involved in this chapter means that a comprehensive history of every tribe involved is simply impossible. What we can achieve, however, is a look into how the native peoples

of the western United States adjusted to and resisted the encroachment of the settlers from the east and the south, and how the Indians of these territories shared common styles of warfare as well as exhibiting some tribal peculiarities.

EXTERMINATION IN THE WEST

We start our analysis with the tribes of California and the Great Basin who, like the Southwestern tribes dealt within the previous chapter, faced encroachment into their territory from Spanish, Mexican and American settlers (see the feature box opposite for a list of major representative tribes in these areas).

Native American history in California stretches back at least 10,000 years. European intrusions, however, began in the sixteenth century with sporadic Russian, Spanish, Portuguese and English explorations. It was the Spanish, however, with their burgeoning empire to the south, who initially had the greatest impact upon the Californian Indians.

The Spanish

In the late eighteenth century, Spanish missionaries began to establish strings of missions along the Californian coastline. In customary fashion, the Spanish brought with them a terrible range of European diseases, which inflicted massive mortality upon many Native American tribes, achieving through biology what the soldiers could not achieve through force of arms. The word of God preached by the missionaries was heavily supported by the arms of man – Franciscans went out into the wilderness supported by intimidating bodies of heavily armed soldiers, just in case their scripture didn't carry

MAJOR GREAT BASIN TRIBES			MAJOR CALIFORNIA INDIAN TRIBES		
Bannock	Chemehuevi	Washoe	Kato	Maidu	Miwok
Mono	Northern Paiute	Panamint	Pomo	Chumash	Wintun
Shoshone	Southern Paiute	Ute	Yokuts	Yuki	Modoc

The position of the Great Basin and Californian Native American tribes meant that they experienced two settler cultures: that of the Spanish and Mexicans pushing up from the south, and that of the American settlers expanding their territories from the east.

enough force. Yet even those who converted to the new religion could expect little comfort, as the French naval officer and explorer Jean François de Galaup, comte de La Pérouse, observed when he visited California in 1786, and saw the life of the neophytes:

'Every day they have seven hours of labour, two of prayers, and four or five on Sundays and feastdays, which are set apart for repose and Divine worship. Corporal punishment is inflicted upon the Indians of both sexes who fail in their religious exercises; and several offences – for which in Europe the punishment is left to the hand of Divine justice – are punished here with irons. From the moment that a neophyte is baptized, it is the same as if he had taken perpetual vows; and, if he should escape from the mission, and take refuge among his relations in their Indian villages,

he is summoned three times to return. If he refuses, the missionaries apply for the authority of the governor, who dispatches soldiers to drag him from the bosom of his family and take him back to the missions, where he is sentenced to receive so many lashes. These Indians are of so timid a character, that they never make any opposition to those who thus violate every human right ...'

– *La Pérouse* (1786)

La Pérouse was not entirely accurate in saying that the Californian Indians 'never make any opposition', however. Native resistance to the muscular Spanish Christianity did take some active forms. The first mission established in California, at San Diego in 1769, was attacked by Kumeyaay Indians within weeks

▲ **A Jesuit priest attempts to convert Native Americans, under the coercive presence of Spanish soldiers. The effort to impose Christian religion did little but alienate the Indians, and push them to military action.**

◀ **The Mohave desert. Despite the austere nature of the terrain in this part of the world, several Indian tribes could comfortably operate here, including the Mohave and the Yavapai.**

of its foundation, and it was entirely destroyed in 1775. Attacks widened to the Spanish population, especially when the Native Americans saw their lands trampled and their crops eaten by Spanish cattle. On 17 July 1781, for example, Kw'tsa'n and Mohave warriors attacked a Spanish settlement and killed 131 people. Other Indians who avoided conversion, or had escaped, banded together in guerrilla alliances in the San Joaquin Valley, making raids for horses and attacking the Spanish military and settlements.

In the end, it was the Mexicans rather than the Native Americans who overthrew the mission system in California. In 1823, following the Mexican War of Independence, Mexico took over the governance of California, and quashed clerical authority. For the Native Americans, the ascent of the Mexicans simply brought new levels of threat.

The Mexicans set about appropriating important tribal territories and, as a result, the Indian resistance grew more ferocious. The Miwoks and Yokuts in particular began a campaign of raiding Mexican settlements and trade routes; such was their effect that the Mexican government in the area ordered the establishment of forts in the interior to try to control them. Epidemics further crippled the Native American capacity to resist, and resulted in shocking reductions in population. In a period of around 70 years prior to the absorption of California into the United States, the population of the Californian Indians was reduced by at least 50 per cent.

American Intervention

The Mexican–American War of 1846–48 once again transformed the fortunes of the California Indians. With the American victory, what had been the Mexican territory of Alta California was annexed by the United States, although at the time of the takeover the settler population of California was a mere 15,000 people. The demographics would change profoundly when gold was

MOHAVE WARRIOR
The Mohave Indians tended to dress with extreme simplicity – this warrior wears nothing more than a loincloth, small feather headdress and regular lines of ochre war paint. In battle, some Mohave were seen wearing a basic form of body armour, consisting of braided vines.

discovered in the hills of the Sierra Nevada in the late 1840s, resulting in the influx of more than 100,000 fortune-hunters in one year alone. The scene was set for a particularly brutal episode in the history of Indian–American relations. Tough-minded waves of settlers made the hunting and killing of Indians a near-sport, seeing the indigenous peoples as a threat to their gold prospecting and new way of life. The Indian tribes responded with the occasional murder, or with theft of livestock belonging to the settlers, but these actions incited truly disproportionate responses by the Americans. One settler, Dryden Lawson, recounted in 1860 that '… in 1856 the first expedition by the whites against the Indians was made … these expeditions were formed by gathering together a few white men whenever the Indians committed depredations on their stock; there were so many expeditions that I cannot recollect the number … we would kill on average fifty or sixty Indians on

▲ **Alaska Territory, 1897. Five Chilkat porters pose with a miner and two oxen on the Dyea Trail, located at the head of the Chilkoot Trail. By this point in history, many of the West Coast Indians had been assimilated into settler culture.**

a trip … frequently we would have to turn out two or three times a week.'

It has been estimated that 100,000 Indians were killed in California during the gold rush years. Genocide was sanctioned at the highest levels – in September 1859, the California governor John Weller actually commissioned an Indian-killer named Walter Jarboe to slaughter Indians indiscriminately – men, women and children. In the same year, the theft of a high-value stallion by Yuki Indians resulted in the massacre of 240 of their number in reprisal. Those not immediately killed were forced into the Round Valley Reservation established in 1854, where they were murdered, raped and assaulted with impunity.

SETTLER ATROCITIES

In 1860, the California legislature established the Joint Special Committee on the Mendocino Indian War (a settler–Indian conflict of 1859) to investigate alleged atrocities against Native Americans. The following extracts of the report illustrate the extreme nature of the violence against the Indians:

'Many of the most respectable citizens of Mendocino County have testified before your committee that they kill Indians, found in what they consider the hostile districts, whenever they lose cattle or horses; nor do they attempt to conceal or deny this fact. Those citizens do not admit, nor does it appear by the evidence, that it is or has been their practice or intention to kill women or children, although some have fallen in the indiscriminate attacks of the Indian *rancherias*. The testimony shows that in the recent authorized expedition against the Indians in said county, the women and children were taken to the reservations, and also establishes the fact that in the private expeditions this rule was not observed, but that in one instance, an expedition was marked by the most horrid atrocity; but in justice to the citizens of Mendocino County, your committee say that the mass of the settlers look upon such act with the utmost abhorrence ... Accounts are daily coming in from the counties on the Coast Range, of sickening atrocities and wholesale slaughters of great numbers of defenseless Indians in that region of country. Within the last four months, more Indians have been killed by our people than during the century of Spanish and Mexican domination...'

▲ **Members of the Southern branch of the Paiute tribe, camped near Mendocino, 1876. They live in 'wickiups' – huts of stick and brush fastened to poles made from willow trees.**

Nor was the escalating war between the Indians and the settlers confined to California, but indeed it spread up the whole of the western United States.

Wider War

American settlers began to reach the Plateau/Great Basin area during the early 1800s. The area was rich ground for mining, particular for gold, silver and copper. As in the case of California, the influx of settlers resulted in inevitable conflict with the native inhabitants, and the experience of the Shoshone Indians was typical.

The Shoshone inhabited the Great Basin around the Rocky Mountains, and their isolated existence suffered a rude shock when they encountered the Europeans during the 1840s. The voracious appetite of the settlers for the local wildlife led to serious hunger among the tribe. By the early 1860s, the Shoshone people had had enough and in 1862 they, along with the Bannock and Paiute tribes, launched a campaign against the settlers in California and Oregon.

The primary tactics of the Shoshone and their allies were raiding and ambushes, typical targets being miners walking woodland trails, wagon trains and stagecoaches. Eventually the Federal Government responded, pulling troops away from the demands of the American Civil War that had been raging for two years by this point. The main tool of enforcement was Colonel Patrick Connor's 1st California Cavalry, which had established a base at Fort Douglas near Salt Lake City. In January 1863, Connor set out into the freezing Midwestern winter in an operation to crush the

RAIDING TACTICS

Indian raiding tactics relied on simultaneously attacking all the major parts of an enemy camp. The raiders would typically spread through the camp at first light, then trigger the attack through a war shout. The goal of the raid could range from inflicting a few casualties through to stealing horses.

northwestern Shoshone, who were led by a warrior chief called Bear Hunter. The snowy conditions probably helped mask the approach of Connor's force, which discovered Bear Hunter's camp along the Bear River. Connor immediately launched a cavalry assault, which was initially repelled, but then the Americans managed to surround and overrun the Indian village, precipitating a horrible massacre of possibly as many as 400 of the Shoshone, the soldiers not discriminating between the victims, regardless of age and gender.

The defeat of Bear Hunter was a prelude of things to come. Connor won similar victories over other Shoshone groups and by the autumn the war was

▲ Bear River, the site of a major engagement between US soldiers and the Shoshone tribe in 1863. The US troops overran a Shoshone village, then massacred up to 400 people.

SHOSHONE TREATY, 1863

The following are Articles 1 and 2 of the treaty concluded between the United States of America and the Shoshone Indians on 1 October 1863:

ARTICLE 1

Peace and friendship shall be hereafter established and maintained between the Western Bands of the Shoshone nation and the people and government of the United States; and the said bands stipulate and agree that hostilities and all depredations upon the emigrant trains, the mail and telegraph lines, and upon the citizens of the United States within their country, shall cease.

ARTICLE 2

The several routes of travel through the Shoshonee country, now or hereafter used by white men, shall be forever free, and unobstructed by the said bands, for the use of the government of the United States, and of all emigrants and travellers under its authority and protection, without molestation or injury from them. And if depredations are at any time committed by bad men of their nation, the offenders shall be immediately taken and delivered up to the proper officers of the United States, to be punished as their offences shall deserve; and the safety of all travellers passing peaceably over either of said routes is hereby guaranteed by said bands. Military posts may be established by the President of the United States along said routes or elsewhere in their country; and station houses may be erected and occupied at such points as may be necessary for the comfort and convenience of travellers or for mail or telegraph companies.

▲ A group of Ute Indians on the war path against the settlers, c.1869. The Ute tribe was part of the Shoshone Nation, which ranged from Colorado and Utah South to New Mexico and Arizona.

essentially over. Another American victory was achieved by a commander we encountered in the last chapter, General George Crook, who during the 'Snake War' (1866–68) took on the Northern Paiute Indians (known by the settlers as the Snake Indians) of the Pacific Northwest. Crook was one of the new breed of military commanders who recognized that conventional tactics were often unsuited to fighting Indians. For example, Kessel and Wooster point out that Crook 'was an avid student of Indian tactics and often used them in his campaigns against hostile

bands. During the course of the Snake War, he used Shoshone auxiliaries and traded his horses and wagons for pack mules. The mule was an animal well suited to negotiating difficult terrain, thus allowing the army better mobility' (Kessel and Wooster, 2005).

Crook's specially formed 23rd Infantry overwhelmed the Paiute through a combination of pursuits and minor battles. As with the Apache tactics described in the previous chapter, Crook's tactical policy served to wear down the Paiute over a prolonged period – he fought a total of 49 minor battles against the Indians before they finally relented and surrendered in July 1868.

The Modoc War and Final Defeat

The 1860s and the 1870s saw the final defeat of Indian armed resistance to the settlers in California. One of the final passionate stirrings of the Native American warrior spirit occurred in the Modoc War of 1872–73. Although the Modoc tribe of northern California and southwestern Oregon had a belligerent reputation, they were generally on reasonable terms with the local settlers. The Modocs had signed a peace treaty with the

▲ General George Crook, the commander of US Army troops during the Snake War (1866–68). Crook had served with distinction in the US Civil War (1861–65) and was involved in the the Great Sioux War of 1876–77. He fought the Lakota at the Battle of the Rosebud.

▶ 'Captain Jack', 1873. Actually named Kientopoos, Jack was best known for the killing of General Edward Canby during negotiations in the Modoc War (1872–73), an act for which he was eventually caught and hanged.

▲ **A vivid portrayal of an action during the Modoc War of 1872–73. Difficult terrain was one of the Modoc's greatest assets during the conflict, not only providing hiding places for the Indians, but also protecting them from US firepower.**

settlers in 1864 after a period of violence, and had moved onto a reservation with the Klamath Indians, traditional enemies of the Modoc. However, a Modoc warrior leader, 'Captain Jack' Kientopoos, caught the current during the rise of the Ghost Dance religion and rejected life on the reservation, leading a group of followers out from the reservation and back into the wilderness.

For the US authorities, Captain Jack's behaviour was unacceptable, and US Army troops under Brigadier General Edward Canby finally tracked down the renegade band to the 'Stronghold', a rocky lava bed at Tula Lake in northern California, which formed an almost impregnable natural barrier. Canby put down heavy artillery fire and made several assaults, but these resulted in little more than adding to the American casualty count (nine dead and 28 wounded on the first

day). Worse was to come for the Americans. An attempt at diplomacy resulted in a meeting between Captain Jack and Canby on 11 April 1873, during which Jack proceeded to shoot and stab Canby to death. Jack and his men fled back to the Stronghold.

Modoc confidence was now running high. On 26 April, a Modoc group headed by the warrior leader 'Scarfaced Charley' ambushed an Army reconnaissance group of 85 men, including some Indian scouts. In the battle that followed, 25 of the soldiers were killed for few (possibly no) Indian losses. Yet although the Modoc seemed to have the tactical advantage,

▲ **The Modoc finally surrender, emerging from the lava beds that were their refuge. By the time the war ended, less than 200 Modoc had survived, and they headed out to reservations in Indian Territory.**

strategically their days were numbered. The Modoc band numbered only some 45–90 people, while the US poured in more troops. Evading such troops was exhausting and slowly Modoc morale and numbers withered. Finally, US troops under the command of the prominent Civil War veteran William Tecumseh Sherman forced the remaining Modoc warriors into either dispersal or surrender. Captain Jack was captured and hanged for Canby's murder in 1873.

Peace Policy and Subjugation

By the time the Modoc War ended in 1873, the Native Americans of the United States had already experienced four years of President Ulysses S. Grant's so-called 'Peace Policy', an attempt to provide a lasting

▶ **Paiute natives sit for the camera in this late nineteenth-century photograph. Apart from bows, they have few weapons – the supplies of firearms to Western Indians was extremely limited.**

solution to conflict between the settlers and the Indians. In November 1869, Jacob D. Cox, Grant's Secretary of the Interior, wrote an annual report outlining the key objectives and intentions of the Peace Policy. His description of the effects of settlement, spoken with pride rather than regret, are significant for this book as a whole:

'The completion of one of the great lines of railway to the Pacific coast has totally changed the conditions

under which the civilized population of the country come in contact with the wild tribes. Instead of a slowly advancing tide of migration, making its gradual inroads upon the circumference of the great interior wilderness, the very center of the desert has been pierced. Every station upon the railway has become a nucleus for a civilized settlement, and a base from which lines of exploration for both mineral and agricultural wealth are pushed in every direction. Daily trains are carrying thousands of citizens and untold values of merchandise across the continent, and must be protected from the danger of having hostile tribes on either side of the route.'

– Cox (1869)

Cox's description of expanding US settlement would make sobering reading to those contemporary Native Americans who could understand the language.

▶ **Mendocino County, California, 1890. Workers lay railroad track to support logging trains. The railroads not only brought more land-hungry settlers to the west, but also resulted in the deforestation of Native American lands.**

The 'slowly advancing tide of migration' has an inexhaustible feel, and the development of the railway makes it clear that even the remotest areas would come under American jurisdiction. Cox continued his document by reflecting on the need to control the Native American population for the protection of the settlers. He explained how the government had two principal aims:

'First, the location of the Indians upon fixed reservations, so that the pioneers and settlers may be freed from the terrors of wandering hostile tribes; and, second, an earnest effort at their civilization, so that they may themselves be elevated in the scale of humanity, and our obligation to them as fellow-men be discharged.'

– Cox (1869)

Just 20 years after Cox made this declaration, the objectives of the Peace Policy were essentially complete. During the 1890s, the frontier was declared officially 'closed', all of the United States having been explored apart from some pockets of Alaska. The Indian tribes were largely confined to demoralizing reservations or restricted areas. The settler conquest of the Native American peoples was now complete, but we will now look at how the Indians of the west managed to sustain some level of military resistance even against the tide of inevitable defeat.

WEAPONS AND ARMOUR

Regarding traditional weaponry, the Western Indians used the familiar range of spear, club and missile arms that we have described elsewhere in this book, with some regional differences. For example, Indian tribes of California and the Great Basin/Plateau regions were known for firing poisoned arrows from their bows, the poisons having been developed over the centuries for hunting game. The poisons used a mixture of ingredients, and carried with them varying degrees of lethality. Sometimes the poisons were extracted from plants such as (in the case of California Indians) the Giant Horsetail Fern, American Pepper Plant or Turkey Mullen. In other cases, concoctions were brewed from animal poisons or the process of putrefaction. The Western Mono and the Southeastern Yavapai made particularly aggressive poisons by stuffing a deer's liver with the toxic parts of rattlesnakes and spiders then either cooking it slowly over a fire or leaving it out in the sun to putrefy. When the time was right, the Indian warriors would dip the tips of their spears and arrows in the caustic organ, then store them in special quivers or holders out of the reach of children. The efficacy of this poison was impressive but slow-working – typically it would take an injured deer about 24 hours to drop dead from the effects. Some accounts refer to settler soldiers dying two days after receiving little more than a minor scratch from such a poisoned arrow.

Other poisons made by the California Indians would not disgrace the pages of a manual on witchcraft. David E. Jones, author of *Poison Arrows: North American Indian Hunting and Warfare* describes one poison made by the Atsugewi tribe that consisted of:

'... a deer pancreas, the gall of a coyote, the air bladder of a fish, red paint, and rattlesnake teeth. The concoction was then mixed in a mortar and permitted to rot before being applied to the arrow or spear points. Another Atsugewi informant told of a method of creating poison in which rattlesnake heads and chopped-up roots of wild parsnip were put in a skin with a handful of arrow points, and allowed to rot before attaching them to arrows.'

– Jones (2007)

▲ A Mohave native with bow and arrows. A classic Western Indian bow type was a yew bow backed with a very thin layer of sinew, to increase the reflex power when the bow was released. Juniper, hickory and ash were also used.

Rattlesnake and plant poisons were found in Native American warfare throughout the western United States, although sometimes a poison could simply involve dipping the point of a spear or arrow in rotted meat or excrement, thereby inducing tetanus in the victims.

Bows

The bows of the Western Indians largely conformed to the models already seen in this book. Along the western coastline, self-bows made of yew, juniper, hickory or ash were the most common style, these typically ranging in length from 91–142cm (36–56in), although bows made at the extreme top end of the scale tended to be rarer and used only for long-range hunting and warfare. Arrow shafts were made from witch hazel, dogwood, viburnum and reed, and the points from obsidian, flint or steel.

In the Rocky Mountains range, and in the Great Basin/ Plateau territories, bows were often made from yew wood imported from further west, but often the problems of sourcing good bow woods in these regions meant that the tribes constructed composite bows using the horns of sheep or buffalo. One interesting feature seen in Western bows is a type of 'silencer'. A major constituent part of the Western Indian diet was deer, a creature easily frightened by the slightest noise. When hunting deer, it was often found that the animal would flinch and start at the sound of a bow being released, and move before the flying arrow could strike it.

To deaden this noise, special dampers made from soft mink or otter fur were tied around the tip of the bow, nestling around the point where the bowstring attached to the bow. When the bow was fired, these dampers suppressed the 'twang' of the string, eliminating the prior warning to the prey. These dampers also proved useful in subsequent conflict with the settlers.

While accuracy of fire was rarely a problem for the Native Americans, having adequate supplies of arrows was another matter. Unlike mass-produced ammunition, arrows required investment of time and skill to produce, and hours or days of careful arrow manufacture could be expended in minutes of combat. Such is evident in an account by Sigismundo Taraval, a Jesuit missionary who worked in Baja California during the 1730s and 1740s, and often experienced the hostility of the Native Americans to his religious objectives. In this extract from his *Indian Uprising in Lower California, 1734–1737*, Taraval describes an attack by local Indians on his group of missionaries, soldiers and allied Indians:

'From the start they hurled endless stones and arrows. Our men, in turn, fired only spasmodically, since the natives were so well situated that we could inflict but little damage. In fact, the natives who were hiding were so well concealed that they could be seen only at the instant when they shot arrows, for afterwards they immediately crouched down …

The fight lasted as long as the arrows lasted. I had warned our Indians not to shoot, since the sooner the enemy exhausted their arrows, the sooner would the attack, danger, and anxiety be over. This was exactly what happened, for within one-half hour the rebels had run out of arrows, although our men had not returned their fire, and so they were forced to withdraw precipitately.'

– *Taraval* (1967)

It is impossible to tell in this extract whether the Indian rebels were using string dampers or not, but it certainly seems that the fact that they could only be identified when standing to fire meant that their practice of cover and concealment was excellent. Unlike many other Indian battles we have seen in this book, however, fire discipline seems less strict,

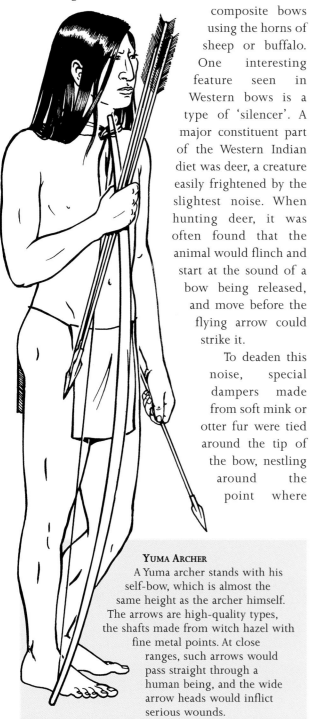

YUMA ARCHER
A Yuma archer stands with his self-bow, which is almost the same height as the archer himself. The arrows are high-quality types, the shafts made from witch hazel with fine metal points. At close ranges, such arrows would pass straight through a human being, and the wide arrow heads would inflict serious wounds.

especially as the enemy was not returning fire. The attack faltered because the men simply ran out of ammunition and were unable to prosecute their attack any further. It is hard to imagine Geronimo, for example, making such a mistake (see Chapter 4).

Ammunition supply was not only a problem in relation to arrows. The Western Indians did have firearms, but as they were mainly captured from the settlers, there was no standardization in ammunition types. During the Battle of Bear River (see above), one of the reasons behind the Shoshone defeat was that they ran out of musket balls. During the battle some Indians were observed attempting to cast new shot, and after the battle the dead were even found still clutching their bullet moulds.

Spears, Blades and Clubs

In addition to bows, the Western Indians carried an age-old assortment of spears, clubs and blades. The oldest traditional type of blade weapon was the obsidian knife. The edge of the obsidian was knapped with a piece of antler or another stone until it took an extremely sharp edge.

Although an obsidian blade was easily damaged, until the introduction of metal blades it gave similar cutting capability, and hence was useful in both war and for hunting. It also, according to this US

▲ Paiute Indians sit in their native terrain with bows and arrows. Between 1860 and 1868, the Paiute fought a bitter war with the American settlers. In one action in 1860, the Paiute killed some 70 US Army soldiers, trapped in an ambush along a narrow trail.

Government report of 1806, could have ceremonial and spiritual significance.

Obsidian was used widely for all manner of weapons, including arrowheads, but its properties as

▲ A Hupa Indian waits patiently for a fish to appear. The Hupa lived in the Hupa Valley, California, and by the early nineteenth century their numbers had dropped to less than 1000 individuals.

a weapon material were questionable. On the one hand, it could undoubtedly achieve a very sharp edge and so made a lethal cutting tool. On the other hand, it was extremely brittle and could shatter easily. Ironically, sometimes this brittle quality was a positive advantage – an obsidian knife or arrowhead stuck in a victim might shatter into several shards, none of which could easily be removed.

In terms of clubs, the most popular varieties were simply knobbed sticks made from suitable hardwoods. The Western Indians also used throwing sticks in hunting and in warfare. These were largely the same as the regular clubs but might be made from heavier woods, such as mahogany, to ensure that they brought down their targets on impact.

FORTIFICATIONS

We have already seen how the Eastern Indians constructed some impressive fortifications. The situation in the west was more varied, however, and depended largely upon the terrain and the type of tribe. In the California area, Native American fortifications were actually relatively rare, mainly on account of the high mobility involved with the hunter-gatherer lifestyle. A select few Californian tribes built simple fortifications consisting of trenches and lodges dug into the earth and covered with earth or plant materials.

Fortification building in the Plateau/Basin regions was similarly basic, typically a combination of trenches working in combination with protective breastworks. *Ad hoc* fortifications and barricades could be constructed in sudden emergencies, using whatever materials and landscape features were in the vicinity.

'SO, TOO, THE YUROK AND HUPA INDIANS OF CALIFORNIA, AS WELL AS SOME OF THE TRIBES OF OREGON, HAVE VERY LARGE SPEARHEADS OR KNIVES, WHICH ARE NOT DESIGNED FOR USE, BUT ONLY TO BE PRODUCED ON THE OCCASION OF A GREAT DANCE. THE LARGER WEAPONS ARE WRAPPED IN SKIN TO PROTECT THE HAND; THE SMALLER ONES ARE GLUED TO A HANDLE. SOME ARE SAID TO BE 15 INCHES [38CM] LONG. THE OREGON INDIANS BELIEVED THE POSSESSION OF A LARGE OBSIDIAN KNIFE BROUGHT LONG LIFE AND PROSPERITY TO THE TRIBE OWNING IT.'

– US GOVERNMENT (1806)

David Jones quotes explorer E.M. Harmon, who in the mid-1940s wrote about a Ute fortification he discovered in Colorado. Local people informed Harman that it had originally been built when a Ute hunting party, which included women and children, was suddenly faced with a sizeable force of Cheyenne and Arapaho raiders. Apparently the construction was of such strength that the much larger group of raiders was unable to penetrate it through direct attack, and eventually retreated. Harmon describes the fortification as follows:

'On the crest of a timbered knoll sloping down to the Fraser River a short distance from the town of Granby, there is what apparently must have been a fort at some time. The side of the knoll away from the river is supported by a ledge of sandstone, forming a perpendicular wall or cliff some fifty or sixty feet [15–18m] in height, from the top of which the crescent-shaped barricade, composed of rocks and rotted logs, enclosed a clear space of less than half an acre [0.2ha] in extent.'

– Harmon (1945)

These types of improvised fortifications were admirable works of defence to build while actually under attack. Yet as the Indians clashed increasingly with the settlers rather than one another, any form of static defensive structure became inadvisable, as it would merely serve to contain the Indians for the firepower of the Europeans.

In fact, on the whole, the supply of firearms to Native Americans in the west was more restricted than was the case further east, particularly in the California area during its 'extermination phase', when any trade in firearms to the Indians was strictly prohibited. The Indians would have to fall back on their native hunting skills if they were to win small victories in a much larger war.

BATTLE TACTICS

Compared to the Native Americans of the opposite coastal zone, the populations of Western Indians, particularly in the California area, were often small. A limited population base, at least in the pre-contact phase of their existence, tended to produce extremely formalized styles of combat, structured so as to produce light casualties that didn't threaten the integrity of a tribe. Inter-tribal conflict was generally expressed through the prearranged 'standing line' tactics that we have seen in other chapters.

Formal Warfare

A good example of this type of warfare is seen in the sixteenth century in a clash between the Kato and Yuki tribes of northern California, who fought a series of battles over rights to access an obsidian mining site. Rights over locations where obsidian was in plentiful supply could be fiercely contested, and brought the Yuki and Kato into conflict on several occasions. In one incident, a Kato woman was killed and beheaded by Yuki warriors.

Such was not an unusual fate in clashes between the tribes – the Kato also practised beheading, the heads of the defeated being taken back to the village where they were boiled and the entire scalp removed as a trophy of battle. On this occasion, the killing was a catalyst for a formal battle, to which the Kato invited the Yuki via messengers.

A location for the fight was agreed, and a smoke signal raised on the day of battle to indicate the time. The subsequent engagement was strictly controlled, with lines of warriors advancing to within bowshot of one another and shooting showers of arrows at the enemy ranks. Observers stood to one side and periodic pauses in the action gave the tribal chiefs an opportunity to make a count of the dead and wounded. The war was played out in this fashion over several separate days, with gaps of as much as 10 days between each engagement, only coming to a close when one side had reached a defined level of casualties that effectively classified it as the loser in the overall battle.

An interesting outcome of the battle, however, was that the side that 'won' the war was actually then obliged to pay compensation to the losers for the destruction of persons or property. Jones notes that 'this custom created a dichotomous situation in which the military winners often became the economic losers' (Jones, 2004).

Such an arrangement probably had a limiting effect on the number of conflicts fought between the Native American tribes, as even victory brought penalties and in hard times such must have been a strong disincentive to fight.

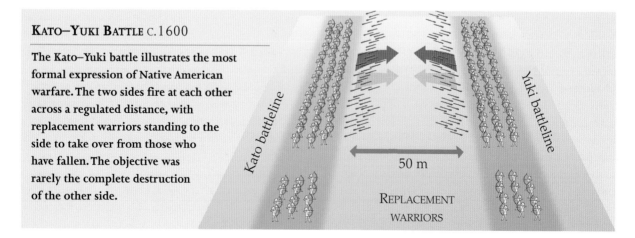

KATO–YUKI BATTLE C.1600

The Kato–Yuki battle illustrates the most formal expression of Native American warfare. The two sides fire at each other across a regulated distance, with replacement warriors standing to the side to take over from those who have fallen. The objective was rarely the complete destruction of the other side.

Kato battleline

Yuki battleline

50 m

REPLACEMENT WARRIORS

Counting Coup

One aspect of Native American warfare that we have not so far considered is the practice of 'counting coup'. This is most commonly associated with the Plains Indians, although it was actually practised to various degrees amongst tribes throughout North America, particularly in the Great Basin/Plateau regions. Counting coup basically involved touching an enemy during a battle then making an escape, this act bringing the warrior honour and reputation for bravery amongst his peers and tribe, as well as illustrating daring, speed and ingenuity.

Note that counting coup did not actually involve harming the enemy warrior; he was simply touched with the hand or with a special coup stick designed for the purpose. Coup sticks were extensively adorned with feathers, fur, scalps, bones and other declaration, and had magical connotations akin to those of a wand. When a warrior returned from battle, he would tap the coup stick against a special pole stuck in the ground in

▲ **Indian warriors in battle count coup on horseback. Touching the enemy with a coup stick could signify bravery as much as the act of killing an enemy in battle, and testified to the swift horsemanship of the warrior.**

the village, the noise marking his victory. There was also some curious etiquette about counting coup, such as that if the warrior touched by the coup-seeking Indian was subsequently killed by another person, the honour of the coup still went to the person who had first counted coup, not to him who had done the killing. Counting coup is a strange practice to Western military eyes, but probably also had an additional limiting effect on the casualty counts of inter-tribal conflicts.

Guerrilla Warfare

These traditional, formalized styles of warfare naturally had little currency once the Indians came into conflict with the settlers, who placed no value on ostentatious displays of bravery in their extermination also formed the cornerstones of their resistance to the settlers. As with everything, hunting techniques informed the strategies of warfare, particularly in terms of cover, concealment and movement.

Rarely did the Indians of the west actually seek pitched battles with conventional forces. Rather, they preferred to wear away at units with frequent minor attacks, or target exposed and vulnerable settler communities rather than 'hard' military objectives. Contrary to how the settlers perceived attacks on civilians, they were rarely conducted because of cowardice or laziness. Settlers, whether in uniform or not, represented a threat to the Indian way of life. While the Indians could never hope to eliminate the settlers from North America, they could attempt to dissuade them from passing through or exploiting their tribal lands. Unfortunately, the excesses that resulted from such a strategy, often provided the excuse for the settlers to dehumanize the Indians.

Use of Terror

One example of an Indian terror attack occurred in 1859 on the Oregon Trail near Fort Hall, Idaho. One of the survivors of what became known as the Late Massacre at Fort Hall, Milton J. Harrington, made a statement about what occurred to the *Desert News*:

'Our company numbered 19 persons 6 men 3 women and 10 children between 1 and 10 years old. Some of the company was from Michigan and the others from Buchanan County, Iowa. At the last crossing of the Sweet Water, we were advised to travel on Lander's Cuttoff being told that that route was nearer, better feed, and safe from Indian depredations.

Our journey was prosperous until the night of the 2nd when we were selecting our place for camping and were making our camp fires. We were startled at the report of a gun, followed immediately by a number of others. We soon ascertained that our rear wagons, which had not yet arrived in camp, were attacked by the Indians. A boy about 10 years old came running to us and said the Indians had killed his father and were killing all the rest. In a moment's time we were surrounded by the savages, whose hideous yells and constant cracking of their rifles at this moment

▲ A Blackfoot counting coup stick. Coup sticks varied in length from around 30cm (12in) up to 76cm (30in), but generally speaking the shorter the stick, the greater its testimony to the bravery of the user.

policies. Here the Native American tribes of the west had to rely more on guerrilla tactics if they were to survive, let alone win battles.

We have already become familiar with the Indian techniques of evasion, manoeuvre, raiding and ambush in previous chapters, and in the west these

HUNTING TECHNIQUES

Josiah Conder, a geographer who travelled through American territory in the first half of the nineteenth century, made some observations of the ingenuity displayed by the Indians during hunting:

'The Indians make use, however, of another very ingenious artifice to approach the stags, and kill them. They cut off the head of a *venado*, the branches of which are very long; and they empty the neck, and place it on their own head. Masked in this manner, and armed also with bows and arrows, they conceal themselves in the brushwood, or among the high and thick herbage. By imitating the motion of a stag when it feeds, they draw round them the flock, which become the victims of the deception. This extraordinary hunt was seen by M. Costanzo on the coast of the channel of Santa Barbara; and it was seen twenty-four years afterwards, in the savannas in the neighbourhood of Monterey, by the officers embarked in the *galetas* Sutil and Mexicana.'

— Conder (1830)

▲ A Native American moose hunting in the Northwestern territory, c.1880. Note the use of rudimentary wooden skis to get close to the animal to deliver a spear blow.

rendered the scene too horrid for description. Those of us who survived made our escape by taking refuge in some rushes and willows on the bank of the Portneuf where we remained during the night. Next day we started on our journey on foot and after traveling three days on scant rations we came to Lieut. Livingston's company of dragoons who were escorting a party to Fort Walla Walla, Oregon.'

The account illustrates several key points about Indian guerrilla warfare. First, it is evident that the presence of Indians influenced the common routes of travel taken by the settlers, as is apparent from the

▲ **A settler outpost in the Western United States in the second half of the nineteenth century. Such outposts, and the trail routes stretching off into the distance, were common targets for Native American attacks.**

discussion about their route being 'safe from Indian depredations' (implying that many others were not). Second, the Indian attack initially targets the rear of the passing column, a softer opportunity than the head of the column, which benefited from the fact that all eyes faced forward. The full force of the attack is unleashed with tempo and aggression, and only flight and hiding saves the surviving settlers from a gruesome fate. Just how gruesome this could be is described in the rest of Harrington's account:

'After informing the command of our distress, Livingston sent a detachment of nine men with one of our company to pilot them to the place of the massacre. Upon their arrival, they found the dead bodies of 5 persons on the ground out of the 8 that were missing. The dead were horribly mangled and scalped. One little girl five-years-old, had both her legs cut off at the knees. Her ears were also cut off and her eyes were dug out from their sockets and, to all appearances, the girl after having her legs cut off had been compelled to walk on the stumps for the sole purpose of gratifying the hellish propensity of savage barbarity.'

– *Desert News* (1859)

There is good reason not to accept accounts such as this at face value. Stories of Indian atrocities were frequently embellished by the American press, often under the official encouragement of the authorities who wanted to fire up the local population in support of their aggressive anti-Indian policies. There were indeed many well-documented accounts of Indian 'barbarity', but many of these related to the practice of scalping or the torture of prisoners. Although undoubtedly horrifying, battlefield mutilation and the torture of prisoners often had deeper spiritual significance for the Native Americans. As we have seen, scalping produced a physical token of bravery, while some tribes practised beheading as a method of acquiring trophies of war. Regarding the torture of prisoners, this activity was not done without purpose. Amongst some tribes, torture was used almost as a means for gaining respect for enemies – the braver the prisoner was while being tortured, the greater the respect the tribe had for him. This could even help improve his chances of his survival.

▲ A Modoc warrior lifts up the freshly cut scalp from his latest victim. As well as taking scalps, the Western Indians would also take the weapons from the fallen enemy, who were one of their major sources of firearms.

Women and children were undoubtedly killed by Native American warriors, but the account of the girl having to walk on severed legs is questionable. Often children were simply despatched with a blow from a club, the thinking being that they couldn't be left alive as they would be an extra mouth to feed – adopting them would place a strain on the resources of the tribe. Despite this, there were many instances where settler children were indeed adopted into Indian society. Yet whether the account of the atrocities were true or not, they had the desired effect on the settlers – a virulent hatred of the American Indians that enabled extermination policies to thrive.

Of course, civilian settlers were not the only targets of Indian guerrilla warfare. During the Paiute War of 1860, the Nevada Paiute often took on conventional US forces in ambush actions. The war began in a typically sordid fashion, after the rape of two Paiute girls led the Indians in a revenge attack on the Williams Station trading post which killed five settlers. A body of just over 100 settler volunteers were gathered to resolve the situation, commanded by Major William

TLINGIT TOTEM POLE
Totem poles were specific to the tribes of the Northwest Pacific Coast and were typically carved from solid cedar tree trunks. Monumental carving probably dates back centuries in Native American culture, but by the end of the nineteenth century the practice was in steep decline.

Ormsby. Inexperience shone through from the very beginning of the operation when, on 12 May, a group of mounted soldiers galloped after a group of fleeing Paiute. The soldiers had little idea that they were falling into a carefully laid ambush until Indian arrows and bullets began to scythe through their ranks. After an about-turn, the volunteer soldiers became trapped along the trail, where subsequent Paiute ambushes whittled down their numbers even further. By the time the remainder of the column found safety, 42 soldiers were dead and 30 missing.

This pattern of attrition and counter-attrition defined much of the warfare in the west, although in the end, Native American tribes could not resist the overwhelming powers of demographics, disease and the increasing counter-insurgency skills of many US Army commanders. The result was that the odds were so stacked against them that they could not push home any advantage they might have gained.

THE PACIFIC NORTHWEST

The Native Americans of the Pacific Northwest (the territory between northern California and southern Alaska) had a very different culture from those in California or living in the Plateau/Basin territories. Tribes such as the Haida, Tlingit and Chinook generally lived in large, stable and static communities, much of their food coming from either saltwater or freshwater sources. Battles between Northwest tribes were fought for largely the same reasons as they were fought anywhere. Like the Indians further south, the Northwestern Native Americans were subject to encroaching colonization from the sixteenth century onwards, not only from Western Europe but also from Russia, and during the nineteenth century the process of subjection was completed through a familiar pattern of assimilation, violence and disease.

Seaborne Warfare

Coastal living had a dramatic effect on the Northwestern Indian style of warfare. Ambushes and raids were delivered directly from canoes, rather like the Vikings preying on the coastline of Western Europe. Amphibious actions could be very substantial indeed – David Jones

notes that the Kwakwaka'wakw tribe 'delivered hundreds of men to a battle, or more likely ambush, in 50- to 70-foot [15–21m] canoes, each carrying thirty to fifty men. The Northwest Coast people often battled on open water in such canoes.'

The explorer Ross Cox, in his 1832 book *Adventures on the Columbia River*, described the process by which the Chinook Indians (who lived in British Columbia and Washington State) fought with a neighbouring tribe. Cox first sets the scene:

'The great mass of the American Indians, in their warlike encounters, fall suddenly on their enemies,

▲ **The Lewis and Clark expedition confront a canoe of Native American warriors. Generally, Lewis and Clark established good relations with Indians they met, without whom the expedition would have starved.**

and taking them unprepared, massacre or capture men, women, and children. The plan adopted by the Chinooks forms an honourable exception to this system. Having once determined on hostilities, they give notice to the enemy of the day on which they intend to make the attack: and having previously engaged as auxiliaries a number of young men whom they pay for that purpose, they embark in their canoes for the scene of action. Several of their women accompany them on these expeditions, and assist in working the canoes.'

— Cox (1832)

Much like the formalized straight-line battles described earlier, the Chinook Indians make an agreement with the enemy regarding the time and place of the battle. The critical difference comes in the form of deployment. Using canoes, the Chinook row the warriors into battle, taking them directly to the enemy's coastal settlement. Once they arrive, however, the two parties then appear to make concerted efforts to avoid a physical clash.

'On arriving at the enemy's village they enter into a parley, and endeavour by negotiation to terminate the quarrel amicably. Sometimes a third party, who preserves a strict neutrality, undertakes the office of mediator; but should their joint efforts fail in procuring redress, they immediately prepare for action. Should the day be far advanced, the combat is deferred, by mutual consent, till the following morning; and they pass the intervening night in frightful yells, and making use of abusive and insulting language to each other. They generally fight from their canoes, which they take care to incline to

TLINGIT CANOE
Being used for coastal travel as well as on inland waters, Tlingit canoes were very substantial affairs, often capable of holding a dozen men. They were dug-out canoes, produced by hollowing out large cedar and spruce logs. Some of the largest specimens of Northwestern Native American canoes stretched up to 18m (60ft) in length.

▲ A Yurok Indian canoe glides down a river. Note that the construction gives the vessel a particularly shallow draft, ideal for navigating inland rivers. Being dug-out canoes, these craft were very durable, hence they might also be used as barricades from behind which the warriors could fire arrows and throw spears.

one side, presenting the higher flank to the enemy; and in this position, with their bodies quite bent, the battle commences. Owing to the cover of their canoes, and their impenetrable armour, it is seldom bloody; and as soon as one or two men fall, the party to whom they belonged acknowledge themselves vanquished, and the combat ceases. If the assailants be unsuccessful, they return without redress; but if conquerors, they receive various presents from the vanquished party in addition to their original demand. The women and children are always sent away before the engagement commences.'

— Cox (1832)

Several elements of this engagement are particularly fascinating when compared to the other actions studied in this book. From the fact that the warriors 'generally fight from their canoes', it is obvious that the combat takes place close the shoreline, the Indians simply pulling their canoes up onto the shore then placing them on their sides as defensive barriers – we saw similar applications in the fortress-storming techniques of the Eastern Indians. As with so many other formal combats, the action is very much focused on casualty limitation, not least because the warriors appear to be heavily armoured. In fact, the Northwest Indians invested more in the development and wearing of body armour than most other Native American groups.

Northwestern Body Armour

The early accounts of settlers in the Northwestern region reveal very sophisticated types of armour indeed. Tlingit warriors observed in the late eighteenth century, for example, wore entire suits made from wooden slats stitched together with thick cord or rawhide. This flexible system sometimes protected the warrior from his neck to his ankles, and

▲ A Spokane hunting party, armed with clubs, knives, bow and arrows and a percussion cap rifle. Firearms never entirely replaced bows, although bow use did decline dramatically with the use of unitary cartridge guns.

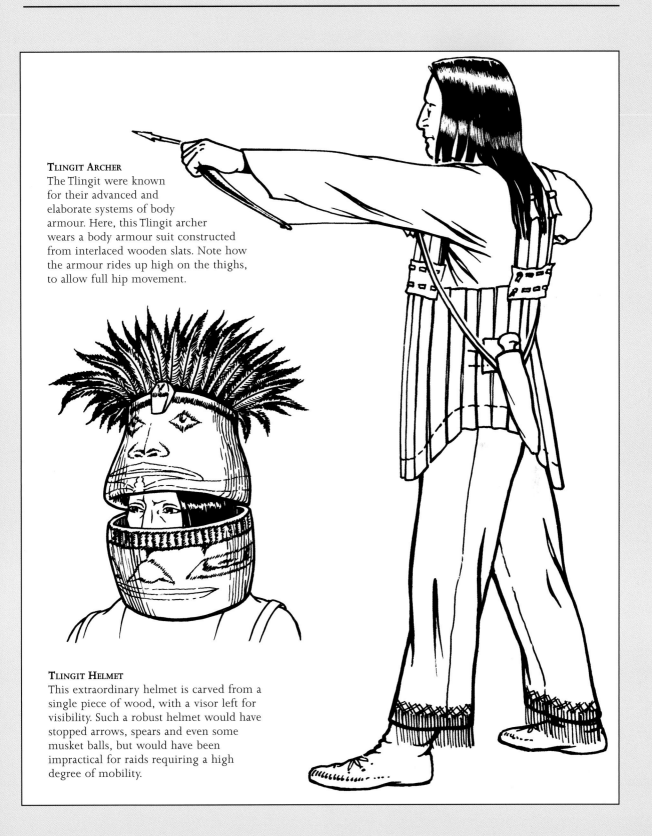

TLINGIT ARCHER
The Tlingit were known for their advanced and elaborate systems of body armour. Here, this Tlingit archer wears a body armour suit constructed from interlaced wooden slats. Note how the armour rides up high on the thighs, to allow full hip movement.

TLINGIT HELMET
This extraordinary helmet is carved from a single piece of wood, with a visor left for visibility. Such a robust helmet would have stopped arrows, spears and even some musket balls, but would have been impractical for raids requiring a high degree of mobility.

▲ A section of a highly decorated Tlingit breastplate, made from deerskin. Although the physical protection afforded by such 'armour' was limited, the decorations were also supposed to give some spiritual protection.

included arm protection also, while the entire head was encased in a solid wood helmet – vision came via a thin eye-slit in the front. Thus protected, the Tlingit would have been hard targets to wound or kill, not least because the wooden armour was worn over the top of a thick leather coat. In fact, stories from around this period state that the Tlingit armour was even capable of stopping a musket ball at relatively close range. A Russian account of 1792 observed that Russian troops engaging the Tlingit fired directly at the helmets to achieve penetration.

The suits were designed to provide for a reasonable degree of movement. Haida armour was similar to that of the Tlingit, and while slats were used for the front and back of the armour, smaller wooden rods were employed at the sides, where they allowed for the body's flexing and bending. Other Northwestern tribes, such as the Tsimshian, created body armour from a combination of layers of elk hide and wooden rods.

Fortifications

The protective mentality of the Northwest Indians is also evident in their strong systems of fortification. The building of fortifications in the Northwest stretches back at least 1500 years, and had developed into a sophisticated art by the time of settler expansion from the sixteenth century. Typically, a fortification was built in a naturally strong position, such as at the summit of a cliff or in elevated, inaccessible and rocky location. Fortifications also took advantage of rivers, which could provide protection for an exposed flank.

The layout of the fortification varied from tribe to tribe, but typically revolved around arrangements of wooden palisades, ditches (both dry and wet) and defensive measures such as spiked branches set in the ground or projecting from the top of the palisades. Palisades might be arranged in single or double rings, and inside the fortification the Indians frequently erected observation/fighting platforms, from which they could scan the surrounding countryside for threats as well as launch spears and arrows at attackers below. The ladders leading up to such platforms could be quickly pulled up if an enemy managed to penetrate the outer defences and enter the fortification.

The scale of the Northwestern fortifications could be impressive. In one fort constructed by the Quinault tribe of coastal Oregon, a total of some 1800 people lived inside a palisaded enclosure built from 5m (16ft)

TLINGIT FORT
This Tlingit fort consists of wood-framed habitations surrounded by a buttressed perimeter wall. In some fortifications, the outer wall would also be surrounded by ditch defensive works, or spiked branches set in the ground as obstructions to attackers. Such fortifications required considerable investment in time and materials to construct, in contrast to the impermanent villages of the nomadic Indian tribes.

high cedar and cottonwood beams. A running walkway set just below the top of the palisade acted as a 360-degree fighting platform.

The Battle of Sitka Sound

One of the most dramatic clashes between the fortified Northwest Indians and the settlers was that which occurred at Sitka Sound, southern Alaska, in 1804 between the Tlingit and the Russians of the Russian–American Company and the Imperial Russian Navy. Animosity between the Tlingit and the Russians stretched back some way. The Russian–American Company had established an outpost just to the north of the Tlingit's hilltop fortification at Sitka, and initial good relations deteriorated as the two peoples clashed culturally and over natural resources. On 20 June 1802, increasing friction came to a head when a large group of Tlingit warriors attacked the Russian outpost, aided by the fact that Western European settlers, who were equally eager to see the back of the Russians, had provided the Tlingit with modern firearms and cannon. The attack was overwhelming, and 150 of the

inhabitants of the outpost (mostly Russian-allied Aleut Indians) were massacred and all the buildings burnt and destroyed.

Understanding full well that Russian reprisals would follow this successful but bloody assault, the Tlingit chose to rebuild their fortification, but this time on a much more substantial basis. Urey Lisyansky, a Russian naval officer who was involved in the impending battle at Sitka, described the resulting construction, set between the sea to its front and woodland to its rear:

'THE FORT WAS AN IRREGULAR SQUARE, ITS LONGEST SIDE LOOKING TOWARDS THE SEA. IT WAS CONSTRUCTED OF WOOD, SO THICK AND STRONG, THAT THE SHOT FROM MY GUNS COULD NOT PENETRATE IT AT THE SHORT DISTANCE OF A CABLE'S LENGTH. … IT HAD A DOOR … AND TWO HOLES … FOR CANNON IN THE SIDE FACING THE SEA, AND TWO LARGE GATES … IN THE SIDES TOWARDS THE WOOD. WITHIN WERE FOURTEEN HOUSES, OR *BARABARAS* … AS THEY ARE CALLED BY THE NATIVES. JUDGING FROM THE QUANTITY OF DRIED FISH, AND OTHER SORTS OF PROVISION, AND THE NUMEROUS EMPTY BOXES AND DOMESTIC IMPLEMENTS WHICH WE FOUND, IT MUST HAVE CONTAINED AT LEAST EIGHT HUNDRED MALE INHABITANTS.'

– LISYANSKY (1814)

The fortification, immune to gunfire, armed with European-supplied cannon and filled with 800 warriors, must have been a challenging prospect indeed for the Russian reprisal fleet on their return to Sitka in 1804 (Lisyansky was the commander of the sloop-of-war *Neva*.) Furthermore, the new fortification had been located at the mouth of the Indian River, which had extensive shallows stretching out into the bay, making approach by Russian ships extremely difficult.

First contact between the Russian force, which consisted of four small Russian warships manned by 150 Russian fur traders, supported by up to 500 Aleuts manning their native kayaks, came on 29 September 1804. The Russians landed some distance from the Tlingit fortification, and initially attempted to

◀ A large Russian naval expedition arrives by boat at Sitka in 1804 under the command of Aleksandr Baranov, the first Russian governor of Alaska. The Russians faced large numbers of Tlingit warriors and had to tackle Native American fortifications whose walls could even withstand naval gunfire.

▲ **Aleksandr Andreyevich Baranov (1746–1819), the Russian trader who rose to become the head of the Russian–American Company, and a force against the Indians of the Pacific Northwest.**

negotiate a peaceful solution. Their efforts were rejected, and battle opened shortly after when the Russians spotted a group of Tlingit warriors transporting gunpowder by canoe back to the fort. The Russians opened fire and hit the canoes, killing all the powder-gathering party in a huge explosion when the gunpowder detonated.

On 1 October, the attack on the Tlingit fortification began in earnest. Having been towed up the shallows by smaller craft, the *Neva* unloaded an artillery detachment onto the beach area to fire on the fort, while the Aleut made a direct assault on the walls. Both of these efforts came to nothing, the fortification walls shrugging off the Russian shot while the Aleuts suffered heavy casualties from Tlingit fire and were forced to retreat back to their kayaks. The Tlingit followed up with a counter-attack, trapping the Aleuts and accompanying Russians in an action that left a dozen of the allied force dead, and several Russian artillery pieces abandoned on the beach.

The second day saw a change of Russian strategy. The commander of the expedition, Alexandr Baranov, had been wounded in the previous day's engagement, so Lisyansky took over. Rather than attempt another costly land attack, Lisyansky opted for three days of naval bombardment against the fortification. Although the shots did not initially penetrate the Tlingit defences, they did start to wear them down and also prevent the Tlingit from conducting operations of their own.

Furthermore, the Tlingit were starting to run out of gunpowder, and they eventually decided simply to abandon the fortification, slipping into the woods under cover of darkness. When the Russians finally entered the fortification, they found that the Tlingit had massacred their own infants and dogs, to prevent their noise giving them away. The Russians then burnt the fortification to the ground.

The battle at Sitka is of a rather different kind to many we having encountered in this book. It proved the strength of the Northwest Indian defences against even a modern naval force, while also illustrating their vulnerability to a prolonged action. Here was the Achilles heel of subsistence communities. While they could be ferocious in the short-term, long-term needs would always limit their ability to prosecute war.

▲ Members of the Tlingit tribe in Klukwan village c.1895, surrounded by totemic carvings. The Tlingit owed much of their culture to Asiatic European origins, hence the oriental allusions in their clothing.

Conclusion

In any analysis of settler–Indian conflict, it must be remembered that demographics played a huge part in the ultimate outcome of wars and campaigns. Total annual immigration into the United States in the second half of the nineteenth century varied from around 150,000 people to more than 500,000, while the Native Americans population growth was limited by natural breeding and also the restricting effects of issues such as loss of hunting grounds and the introduction of foreign diseases. In short, the settlers could make good their losses infinitely easier than the Native Americans. Any Native American campaign was doomed to fail regardless of military success – in the end, they would be overwhelmed by numbers.

Regardless of the outcome, in the process of taking on the settlers the Indians of North America had certainly proved their ingenuity, martial skills,

endurance and adaptability. It was these abilities that led the armed forces of the United States to utilize Indians within regular forces, particularly for their scouting abilities. The end of significant Indian resistance to settler expansion at the end of the nineteenth century did not stop Native Americans entering the ranks of the US military and finding purpose and distinction there.

Rough Riders

In 1898, for example, Indian troops were recruited by Theodore Roosevelt's 'Rough Riders', serving in the Spanish–American War, and during the twentieth century there was no shortage of opportunities for military service. When the United States entered World War I in 1917, some 12,000 Native Americans joined US Army ranks on the battlefields of Europe. Although many of these individuals served in auxiliary roles, large numbers also distinguished themselves in combat. The performance of 600 Choctaw and

◀ Bankston Johnson was a full-blooded Choctaw Indian who served in Theodore Roosevelt's 'Rough Riders' in the late nineteenth century. The Rough Riders was the name for the 1st United States Volunteer Cavalry, raised for service in the Spanish–American War.

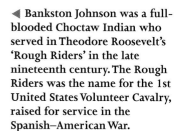

▶ Italy, 1944. Second Lieutenant Ernest Childers, an American Indian from Tulsa, Oklahoma, receives the Congressional Medal of Honor from Lieutenant General Jacob L. Devers (left). The medal was received for Childers having wiped out 32 German machine gun nests near Oliveto, Italy, killing five Germans and capturing one.

Cherokee Indians in the 142nd Infantry of the 36th Texas-Oklahoma National Guard Division, for instance, led to four of them being awarded the Croix de Guerre in honour of their bravery on the battlefield, and many other Native Americans also received US and foreign decorations.

World War II Service

The martial traditions of Native Americans continued in World War II, when more than 44,000 Indians saw service in all aspects of the American military – Army, Marine Corps, Navy, Army Air Force and Coast Guard. The Native American community seemed particularly

▲ Bougainville Island, 1943. Two US Marine Corps Navajo 'code talkers' – signalmen who used a slightly modified version of their native language as a code – send a radio signal during the battle of Bougainville.

motivated to serve during the conflict, as 40 per cent more Native Americans enlisted voluntarily than were drafted, and by 1942, 99 per cent of all Indians eligible for military service had registered themselves. The motivation was reflected in the large numbers of decorations, of every status, bestowed upon Native Americans for bravery in action.

For example, three Native American soldiers of the 45th Infantry Division – Lieutenant Emest Childers (Creek), Lieutenant Jack Montgomery (Cherokee) and Lieutenant Van Barfoot (Choctaw) – all won Medals of Honor for quite astonishing acts of courage. Barfoot, for example, knocked out two German machine-gun nests, took 17 prisoners, destroyed three enemy tanks and physically carried two men to safety during fighting around Anzio.

'Code Talkers'

A particularly distinctive Indian contribution to World War II was that made by the Navajo 'Code Talkers' in the Pacific theatre, while serving with the US Marine Corps (USMC). Philip Johnston, an engineer in the United States, had been in regular contact with the Navajo Indians during his youth.

As an adult he became convinced that the Navajo language was ideal as a basis for a military code (he spoke Navajo fluently), being practically indecipherable to anyone who had not been immersed in its structures and dialects. He proved his point to the US Marine Corps, which was looking to establish secure communications during the Pacific campaign, and from May 1942 the USMC began to recruit Navajo soldiers as 'code talkers'.

▼ Joe Rosenthal's famous flag-raising picture, taken on Iwo Jima in 1945, featured Pima Native American Ira Hayes (far left). Hayes adjusted badly to the fame generated by the photograph, and descended into alcoholism, dying at the age of just 32.

WOODROW W. KEEBLE
The following is the Medal of Honor citation for Woodrow W. Keeble, the first full-blood Sioux Indian to achieve this decoration. He received the award for bravery during his service in the 19th Infantry during the Korean War:

'RANK AND ORGANIZATION: MASTER SERGEANT, U.S. ARMY.

PLACE AND DATE: KOREA, 20 OCTOBER 1951.

MASTER SERGEANT WOODROW W. KEEBLE DISTINGUISHED HIMSELF BY ACTS OF GALLANTRY AND INTREPIDITY ABOVE AND BEYOND THE CALL OF DUTY IN ACTION WITH AN ARMED ENEMY NEAR SANGSAN-NI, KOREA, ON OCTOBER 20, 1951. ON THAT DAY, MASTER SERGEANT KEEBLE WAS AN ACTING PLATOON LEADER FOR THE SUPPORT PLATOON IN COMPANY G, 19TH INFANTRY, IN THE ATTACK ON HILL 765, A STEEP AND RUGGED POSITION THAT WAS WELL DEFENDED BY THE ENEMY.

LEADING THE SUPPORT PLATOON, MASTER SERGEANT KEEBLE SAW THAT THE ATTACKING ELEMENTS HAD BECOME PINNED DOWN ON THE SLOPE BY HEAVY ENEMY FIRE FROM THREE WELL-FORTIFIED AND STRATEGICALLY PLACED ENEMY POSITIONS. WITH COMPLETE DISREGARD FOR HIS PERSONAL SAFETY, MASTER SERGEANT KEEBLE DASHED FORWARD AND JOINED THE PINNED-DOWN PLATOON. THEN, HUGGING THE GROUND, MASTER SERGEANT KEEBLE CRAWLED FORWARD ALONE UNTIL HE WAS IN CLOSE PROXIMITY TO ONE OF THE HOSTILE MACHINE-GUN EMPLACEMENTS. IGNORING THE HEAVY FIRE THAT THE CREW TRAINED ON HIM, MASTER SERGEANT KEEBLE ACTIVATED A GRENADE AND THREW IT WITH GREAT ACCURACY, SUCCESSFULLY DESTROYING THE POSITION. CONTINUING HIS ONE-MAN ASSAULT, HE MOVED TO THE SECOND ENEMY POSITION AND DESTROYED IT WITH ANOTHER GRENADE. DESPITE THE FACT THAT THE ENEMY TROOPS WERE NOW DIRECTING THEIR FIREPOWER AGAINST HIM AND UNLEASHING A SHOWER OF GRENADES IN A FRANTIC ATTEMPT TO STOP HIS ADVANCE, HE MOVED FORWARD AGAINST THE THIRD HOSTILE EMPLACEMENT, AND SKILLFULLY NEUTRALIZED THE REMAINING ENEMY POSITION. AS HIS COMRADES MOVED FORWARD TO JOIN HIM, MASTER SERGEANT KEEBLE CONTINUED TO DIRECT ACCURATE FIRE AGAINST NEARBY TRENCHES, INFLICTING HEAVY CASUALTIES ON THE ENEMY. INSPIRED BY HIS COURAGE, COMPANY G SUCCESSFULLY MOVED FORWARD AND SEIZED ITS IMPORTANT OBJECTIVE. THE EXTRAORDINARY COURAGE, SELFLESS SERVICE, AND DEVOTION TO DUTY DISPLAYED THAT DAY BY MASTER SERGEANT KEEBLE WAS AN INSPIRATION TO ALL AROUND HIM AND REFLECTED GREAT CREDIT UPON HIMSELF, HIS UNIT, AND THE UNITED STATES ARMY.'

▲ Woodrow W. Keeble served with distinction in both World War II and the Korean War. He received his Medal of Honor posthumously in 2008, having been recommended for the medal twice during his Korean War service.

Around 400 Navajo eventually served in this capacity, and while the Japanese were able to break many of the codes used by American battlefield forces, they never came close to penetrating the Navajo system. At the battle of Iwo Jima in 1945, a USMC signals officer, Major Howard Connor, said that 'Were it not for the Navajos, the Marines would never have taken Iwo Jima.'

Postwar Service

After 1945, Native Americans continued to serve with distinction in the American armed forces, in theatres ranging from frozen North Korea to the jungles of Vietnam. It has only been in recent enlightened times, however, that the military contribution of the Native Americans has been fully recognized. In November 2001, President George W. Bush proclaimed the foundation of National American Indian Heritage Month, and in so doing made a very public acknowledgement of Indian service in the US forces, past, present and future:

'As we move into the 21st century, American Indians and Alaska Natives will play a vital role in maintaining our Nation's strength and prosperity. Almost half of America's Native American tribal leaders have served in the United States Armed Forces, following in the footsteps of their forebears who distinguished themselves during the World Wars and the conflicts in Korea, Vietnam, and the Persian Gulf. Their patriotism again appeared after the September 11 attacks, as American Indian law enforcement officers volunteered to serve in air marshal programs.'

When held up against past attitudes of American leaders towards the indigenous peoples – which at times amounted to explicit extermination policies – George Bush's declaration stands in sharp contrast. Although the military history of the Native American peoples prior to the twentieth century is in general a tale of woe, the martial skills of individual tribes and warriors are never to be doubted.

▶ Native American Marines pose on the island of Bougainville, in the Pacific Islands. Far from the days of bows and arrows, they clutch M1 Garand rifles and Reising submachine guns.

BIBLIOIGRAPHY

PRIMARY SOURCES

'A Canadian Campaign, by a British Officer', *New Monthly Magazine* (1827).

Bogoras, Waldemar. *The Chukchee. The Jesup North Pacific Expedition. Memoir of the American Museum of Natural History*, Vol. 7 (1909).

Bryant, Charles S. *A history of the great massacre by the Sioux Indians, in Minnesota: including the personal narratives of many who escaped* (1864).

Cox, Ross. *Adventures on the Columbia River: including the narrative of a residence of six years on the western side of the Rocky Mountains, among various tribes of Indians hitherto unknown: together with a journey across the American continent* (1832).

Conder, Josiah. *The Modern Traveller: A Description, Geographical, Historical, and Topographical, of the Various Countries of the Globe* (1830).

Curtis, Edward S. *The North American Indian*, Vol. 20 (1930).

Denig, Edwin Thompson. *The Assiniboine* (1930).

Gookin, Daniel. 'An historical account of the doings and sufferings of the Christian Indians in New England in the years 1675, 1676, 1677' in *Archaeologica Americana, Transactions and Collections of the American Antiquarian Society*, II (1836).

Harman, Daniel. *A Journal of Voyages and Travels in the Interior of North America* (1922).

Irving, John T. 'VIII. Indian Sketches, taken during an Expedition to the Pawnee and other Tribes of American Indians, *Monthly Review* Vol. III, No.1 (1835).

Irving, Washington. *Astoria: or, Enterprise beyond the Rocky mountains* (1836).

Kane, Paul. *Wanderings of an artist among the Indians of North America: from Canada to Vancouver's Island and Oregon, through the Hudson's Bay company's territory and back again* (1859).

Keim, De Benneville Randolph. *Sheridan's Troopers on the Borders: a Winter Campaign on the Plains* (1825).

Lafitau, Joseph. *Customs of the American Indians Compared with the Customs of Primitive Times*, Vol.2 (1724).

Lewis, Meriwether and William Clark. *Travels to the Source of the Missouri River and Across the American Continent to the Pacific Ocean, Performed by Order of the Government of the United States, in the Years 1804, 1805, and 1806*, Vol. 3 (1815).

Lisyansky, Urey. *A voyage round the world: in the years 1803, 4, 5, & 6* (1814).

Malte-Brun, Conrad. *Universal Geography: Or, A Description of All Parts of the World, on a New Plan, According to the Great Natural Divisions of the Globe....* Vol. 3 (1829).

Murray, Hugh. *An historical and descriptive account of British America...* (1839).

Rowlandson, Mary. *A Narrative of the Captivity and Restoration of Mrs. Mary Rowlandson* (1682).

Schoolcraft, Henry Rowe. *Narrative journal of travels through the northwestern regions of the United States: extending from Detroit through the great chain of American lakes to the sources of the Mississippi River, performed as a member of the expedition under Governor Cass in the year 1820* (1821).

Taraval, Sigismundo. *Indian Uprising in Lower California 1734–1737* (Ayer Publishing, 1967).

Turner, George. *America ...Volume 2 of Traits of Indian Character: As Generally Applicable to the Aborigines of North America* (1836).

Venegas, Miguel. *A Natural and Civil History of California: Containing An accurate Description of that Country, Its Soil, Mountains, Harbours, Lakes, Rivers and Seas, its Animals, Vegetables, Minerals and famous Fishery for Pearls: The Customs of the Inhabitants, Their Religion, Government and Manner of Living...* (1759).

SECONDARY SOURCES

Ewers, John C. *The Blackfeet: Raiders on the Northwestern Plains* (Norman, OK: University of Oklahoma Press, 1958).

Hamm, Jim. *Bows & Arrows of the Native American Indians* (Guilford, CT: Lyons Press, 1989).

Hook, Jason. *The American Plains Indians* (Oxford: Osprey, 1985).

Hook, Jason. *The Apaches* (Oxford: Osprey, 1987).

Johnson, Michael. *American Indians of the Southeast* (Oxford: Osprey, 1995).

Johnson, Michael. *American Woodland Indians* (Oxford: Osprey, 1990).

Johnson, Michael. *Indian Tribes of the New England Frontier* (Oxford: Osprey, 2006).

Johnson, Michael. *Tribes of the Iroquois Confederacy* (Oxford: Osprey, 2003).

Jones, David E. *Native North American Armor, Shields, and Fortifications* (Austin, TX: University of Texas Press, 2004).

Jones, David E. *Poison arrows: North American Indian Hunting and Warfare* (Austin, TX: University of Texas Press, 2007).

Kessel, William and Robert Wooster (eds). *Encyclopedia of Native American Wars & Warfare* (New York: Checkmark Books, 2005).

Lardas, Mark. *Native American Mounted Rifleman 1861–65* (Oxford: Osprey, 2006).

Meed, Douglas V. *Comanche 1800–74* (Oxford: Osprey, 2003).

Parcher Russell, Carl. *Guns on the early frontiers: a history of firearms from colonial times through the years of the Western fur trade* (Lincoln, NE: University of Nebraska Press, 1980).

Starkey, Armstrong. *European and Native American Warfare 1675–1815* (Abingdon: University of Oklahoma Press, 1998).

Taylor, Colin F. *Native American Hunting and Fighting Skills* (London: Salamander, 2003).

WEBSITES

The American West
http://www.americanwest.com/pages/indians.htm

The Pequot War
http://www.pequotwar.com/

American Indians of the Pacific Northwest Collection
http://content.lib.washington.edu/aipnw/index.html

The Bonneville Collection – Nineteenth century images of Native Americans and Soldiers in the American West
http://www.sc.edu/library/digital/collections/bonneville.html

McKenney and Hall Indian Tribes of North America
http://content.lib.washington.edu/mckenneyhallweb/index.html

Native American Treaties and Information
http://ucblibraries.colorado.edu/govpubs/us/native.htm

Library of Congress – Native American History
http://memory.loc.gov/ammem/browse/ListSome.php?category=Native%20American%20History

Native American History
http://www.shmoop.com/native-american-history/

INDEX

Page numbers in *italics* refer to illustrations.